ENGLISH RECUSANT LITERATURE
1558–1640

Selected and Edited by
D. M. ROGERS

Volume 293

GIUSEPPE BIONDO
*A Relation of the Death
of . . . Troilo Savelli*
1620

GUILLAUME DU VAIR
Holy Philosophy
1636

GIUSEPPE BIONDO

*A Relation of the Death
of . . . Troilo Savelli*
1620

The Scolar Press
1976

ISBN o 85967 294 8

*Published and printed in Great Britain by
The Scolar Press Limited, 59-61 East Parade,
Ilkley, Yorkshire and
39 Great Russell Street,
London WC1*

NOTE

The following works are reproduced (original size) with permission:

1) Giuseppe Biondo, *A relation of the death of . . . Troilo Savelli*, 1620, from a copy in the library of Downside Abbey, by permission of the Abbot and Community.

References: Allison and Rogers 112; STC 3134.

2) Guillaume Du Vair, *Holy philosophy*, 1636, from a copy in the library of Heythrop College, by permission of the Librarian.

Reference: Allison and Rogers 290; not in STC.

A
RELATION
OF THE DEATH,
OF THE MOST
ILLVSTRIOVS LORD,

Sig.r Troilo Sauelli,

a Baron of Rome;

Who was there beheaded, in the Caftle of Sant-Angelo, on the
18. of Aprill, 1592.

With a Preface, conteyning diuers particulers, which are wholy neceffary to be
knowne, for the better vnderftanding
of the Relation it felfe.

Domine, quis fimilis tibi? Pfal. 34.

O Lord, who is like to thee?

Permiffu Superiorum, M.DC.XX.

THE
PREFACE
TO
THE READER.

THE *Relati-*
on following,
hath beene
tranſlated in-
to diuers lan-
guages; though not at all
into ours, nor yet ſo carefully,

fully, into others, out of
the true Original *Italian*, as
I could haue wished. The
differences between the co-
pies, which walke vp, and
downe the world, are not
great; sauing, that when
there is question of truth;
and that, concerning a noble subiect; and the same,
accompanyed with variety
of naturall, and liuely circumstance, I cannot find in
my hart, to let any difference goe for small. I haue
therefore, at once, taken
both paynes, and pleasure,
                          to

to draw ftore of copyes into
my hand , and it hath not
beene without fucceffe. For
if I haue not layd hold vpõ
the very firft *Original*, which
was written by the Relatour
himfelfe; I dare fay, that I
am growne very neere it, &
that itis precifely true. And
this *Elogium* I will be bold
to giue to the Difcourfe,
which we haue in hand, that
it hath beene reade in feue-
ral countryes with extreme
auidity. Nay perhaps there
hath not iffued, in many of
thefe laft ages, any one hi-
A 2   ftori-

storicall *Relation*, of a particuler accident, the (a) consideration whereof, hath
more often beene attended
by teares, then this.

The (b) Perſon whome
it concerneth, was a *Baron*
of *Rome*, *Sig.* ʳ *Troilo Sauelli*;
a braunch, which ſprunge
vp, from a root of as noble
bloud, as a moſt certaine
extractiō from the ancient
Romans, could tell how to
make it. His perſon, & the
parts of his generous mind,
are beſt deſcribed in the *Relation* it ſelfe, which followeth;

(a) The
relation
follow-
ing hath
been ſel-
dome
read
without
tender-
nes.

(b) The
birth, &
perſon,
& parts
of this
Noble
Man.

eth ; so that, I will not heere
by putting y ou to paynes ,
preuent the pleasure which
there you wil haue to ouer-
take them . The cause for
which he suffered , is not
specified there at all ; because his ghostly Father was
the penner of this narrati-
on ; and it became not him,
who was the others Iudge
in foro Conscientiæ, to become
his Accuser , *in foro Curiæ* .
For although his crimes
were extant then , and are
so stil vpon *Record*; and that
the penitent did besids (for
A 3 his

his owne greater confufion, and the exaltation of the inuincible Patience, and Mercy of Almighty God) giue his Ghoſtly Father ex-preſſe leaue, to declare his ſinnes to the whole world; the Father yet, would by no meanes accept of that liber-ty; but ſpeaking only in ge-nerall wordes, of ſinne at large; he (c) burieth the par-ticulers in profoūd ſilence, and vnder the ſeale of *Confeſſion*, for reuerence of that holy *Sacrament*, which muſt neuer vpon any termes be defaced.   But

(c) The inuiola-ble ſeale of the Sacra-ment of Confeſ-ſion; & howten-der a good Ghoſtly Father, is, and ought to be.

But I, who am free, will
not confent to haue my
handes tyed vp ; but doe
think it fit to let you know,
that although his yeares
were few, his crimes were
great, & many ; as doth ftil
appeare vpon the *Record* of
his *Proceſſe*. And betweene
the fixteenth, and the eigh-
tenth yeare of his age (till
the former of which tymes,
his vigilant, and holy Mother, was able to keep him
in the difcipline of piety, &
vertue) he fprouted out, into great exorbitances ; and

in

in the Company, and at the head of the (d) *Banditi*, he committed both rapes and murthers, with a most tempestuous, and transported mind. *Omnis* (e) *inimica amicitia, seductio mētis inuestigabilis.* He did too early, cast himselfe into the hands of flatterers, & wicked followers; and they made the way of sinne so smooth to him, as that he could not hold frō sliding through it. Nor was his tender youth so innocent cent

(d) These are men who for murthers, & other extreme insolencyes vse to be banished and proscribed. They were wont in Italy, to go, in great troopes vp and downe, & to infest the passages.

Sixtus *Quintus*, was one of the first, who broke their backe.   (e) The bane which is brought vpon young noble men by ill company.

cent, nor his education so
excellent, but that the
moath, and canker of lewd
company, did soon corrode
it.

Yet euen heerein, was
not his misery so great, as
the (f) mercy of God, vpon
this occasion, was infinite.
His crims were not known,
but by such alone, as would
not easily aduenture to
draw vpon themselues, the
displeasure of so greate a
house as his, by detecting
them. The manner only of
his life, in respect of ex-

(f) It is
proper
to God
alone, to
draw
good
out of
euill.

A 5   cesse,

cesse, and riot, was such, in the exteriour, as wounded his noble, and tender Mother to the very soule. The passages, and proceedinges whereof, are deliuered in the *Relation* it selfe, with so greate tendernes, in the person of her sonne, as strikes the hart of him that reades the wordes. I will not therfore touch that flowre, for feare of strikng off the dew, euery dropp whereof is a pearle. One circumstance only which is not mentioned there, I will

heere

heer expresse, because it wil not faile to serue, towardes the increase of compassion, in all their mindes, who reade this story.

You (g) shall therfore vnderstand, that when the Mother had vsed all other possible endeauours, both diuine and humane, for the reduction, and reformation of her sonne, and all in vaine (for ought that she was able to perceiue) she caused him, for some offences (which yet, were farre from being Capitall) to be

com-

(g) A circumstãce of great importance, towards the mouing of compassion.

(h) This is the chiefe prifon in Rome, as the Tower may be in London.

committed to Caftle (h) *S. Angelo* ; in hope that fuch a difgrace , with the help of tyme , would make him re-turne into hmfelf. To this courfe she was the more encouraged, & in this hope the more confirmed , be-caufe by this reftraint , he would be cut off from that ill company , which was the very peft, and poifon of

(i) Any little en-trance into pu-blique difgrace carryeth danger with it,

his foule. But fee, and won-der at Gods prouidence . He (i) was no fooner in prifon, but the fire of eager oppofition brake forth of their

their hartes, whom, by his
other more enormous info-
lencyes, he had offended ;
for till then, it had beene
smoothered vnder the a-
shes of that respect, and reuerence, which they carryed towards the Dignity, &
Nobility of his house . But
now *publique Iustice* taking
notice of his excesses ; and
Pope Clement the eight, in
the beginning of his *Pontifi-*
cate, being desirous to shew
a strong example, of what
vnpartiall *Iustice*, the world
was to expect at his hands;
(especi-

(especially in repressing,
& extinguishing that afore-
said damned crue of *Banditi*,
who were so pernicious to
the State of *Italy*, and of
whom this yong Lord was
growne a leader) did suffer
the law to passe vpon his
person(for his state was not
confiscated, but went to his
heyres, in bloud) . Being
euen yet therin , more *Iust*,
then *Clement*; though perhaps he would haue been
more *Clement* in pardoning,
then *Iust* in punishing; if
he could , by way of anti-
cipa-

cipation, haue feene the beauty, and brauery of that noble spirit, which deser- ued to liue as longe, as a world can do; as a patterne, of a mind most rarely com- pounded, between perfect Christian piety, and vn- daunted incomparable ma- gnanimity.

But whyleſt the (k) Mother, and the Sonne, are both of them reſtinge now in peace, and glory, as we may piouſly belieue; I know not

(k) This Lady dyed in the year 1611. and was bu- ryed on the 21. of October in the Thea- tines Church at *Sant Andrea della Val- le*; wher ſhe ere- cted ten maſſes to be ſayd e- uery day, for euer. She was of the houſe of the Dukes of *Ceſi*; and ſiſter to the Marqueſſe of *Riano*: her name was *la Signora Flaminia*.

not how, in this particuler, to be silent, concerning the powerfull, and wise, and infinitely good (l) proui-dence, of Almighty God, towardes both these seruan-tes of his. For, by the way of the (m) *Crosse*, he brought the sonne, in a few momen-tes of time, to haue a soule in state of great perfection; and he gaue him, in the last houres of his life, that most happy kind of *Purga-tory*; wherin he might not only suffer, in satisfaction of the diuine *Iustice*, but passe

on

(l) The proui-dence of God, de-serueth to be deeply ponde-red, in this par-ticuler.

(m) The Crosse is the high way to heauen.

on by *merittes*, (all groun-
ded ỿpon the mercy of *Iesus*
Chriſt our (n) Lord (as all
merits are) towards inſtant,
and eternall felicity.

And this he did, by as
contrary meanes, as in the
Ghoſpell he cured a certaine
Blind man, by (o) *caſting durt*
ỿpon *his eyes*. For heer he v-
ſed, the moſt indulgent tender care of the mother, who
loued that Sonne, as her
owne ſoule ; towardes the
bringing that about, which
was indeed, to make him
happy in the end; but in the

(n) No action of man is meritorious, but by the merits and firſt mercy of Iesus Chriſt our Lord.

(o) The omnipotency of God, is not tyed to meanes, but workes his will, how he will.

B   meane

meane tyme, was the occa-
fion of his fuddaine, and re-
proachfull death, whereby
her very hart was to be broken. Taking him fo from
her fight, that fo she might
enioy a glorious fight of
him for euer; & depriuing
her of all humane comforts
(which(for as much as concerned her) were abridged,
& locked vp in him alone)
that fo she might, with contempt of the world, fend
her whole hart vp to hea-
uen, whither now her treafure was gone before; and fo
be

be rewarded , for that tender and entire care, which she had taken, for his pious education .

It (p) matters not much, what the blind , and dull world conceaues ; which placing fayth in fancy ; and religious reafon in the treacherous fenfe of flesh and bloud ; thinkes all that to be mifery , which carryeth the face of paine, or shame, or any difficulty ; and that true happines confiftes in rowing for a whyle in fome boate (q) of mufike, downe

(p) The blind & blocke-headed difcourfe of worldly men .

(q) A fit emblem to fhew the vanity of worldly pleafure.

B 2 the

the tide ; though it carry them foone after , where they are either to be fplit vpon rockes , or fwallowed vp by quick-fandes. Wheras God knowes (yea & men whohaue his grace, are not ignorãt therof)that a courfe of felicity, not interrupted, or checked by contrary windes, is a kind of fortune (for as much as concerneth the next life) which in this, deferueth rather pitty,then enuy ; and that , euer fince the death of Iefus Chrift our Lord , the way of the

Croffe

Croſſe , is (r) not only the more ſafe , but euen the more honorable; and that the pleaſures, and paſtimes of this life , ar but a kind of butterfly, for boyes to play withall; & that the greateſt earthly felicity , that euer was enioyed by man , if it dyed not as ſoone as it was borne (which yet is the or-nary caſe of (s) worldly plea-ſure) at leaſt , if it liued til it could learne to ſpeake , it told as many lies , as it vtte-red wordes ; and charmed them firſt , whom quickly

(r) The croſſe of Chriſt our Lord, hath made miſery, to be-come happy?

(s) World-ly plea-ſure ſpeakes faire , but it lyes.

B 3   after

after, it might lead towards
a precipice.

How defolate, would
a worldling thinke, that
the cafe of *Signor Troylo Sa-*
uelli was, in that night when
he receaued the newes of
his fo inftantely approa-
ching, côtumelious death?
And of that deare Mother
of his, when she heard the
blow was giuen, which parted that head from thofe
shoulders? And (t) yet with
all, is it both well knowne,
that the Mothers loffe of
fuch a fonne, did caft her
                                    much

(t) Af-
fliction,
made
the Mo-
ther, &
the Son,
feeme
mifera-
ble, and
be hap-
py.

much more clofe, vpon an
vnion and fole dependance
for all her comfort, vpon
Almighty God; (wherein
the happines, which we can
haue in this life confifts)
and it is morally certaine,
that the abundant grace of
Contrition, and Charity,
which God infufed into the
hart of the *Sonne*, euen by
the occafion of his very fins
(fo vaftly & infinitely good
is God)did put him inftantly, after his death, into a
ftate fo bleffed, as that the
Pope himfelfe, vnder whom

B 4   he

he died , and thofe *Princes* amongft whom he liued , and all the *Monarches* of the whole world , may be accounted to haue bin miferable, according to their prefent ftate, in refpect of him. Our deare Lord *Iefus* , be eternally thanked (& not only by vs, who know not how to do it well, but by all his holy Angells, and Saintes) for his owne infinite goodnes ; fince he vouchfafes to (u) place the point of his Honour, in fhewing mercyes, and working wonders

(u) He could eafily honour himfelfe otherwife, without any benefit to vs , if he were fo pleafed.

ders vpon man, fo inftantly,
fo fweetely, fo powerfully,
and fo like a God . And for
hauing fuffered, in his owne
facred foule, & body, fuch
defolations, and torments,
as obtained, at the handes
of the eternall Father, not
only the remiffion of our
finnes, (if we will ferue our
felues of the *Sacraments*, and
other remedyes which he
hath left in the bofome
of his holy *Catholike Church*)
þut the adorninge alfo of
our foules, with the inhe-
rent giftes, and graces of

B 5   the

the holy Ghoſt . And yet further , for that he hath knowne , how to make our very ſinnes , and greiuous crimes themſelues , the meanes , ſome times , wherby we obtaine greater graces, then (x) we should haue done , if we had not committed thoſe very ſinnes .

(x) This indeed is a mercy , which may wel become the greatnes of our God.

Let the whole world therfore adore thee , O Lord , and ſing prayſes to thee ; and let all the powers of all ſoules cry out , and ſay with that holy King , and Prophet *Dauid, O Lord who is like to thee ?*

A

A great example, and proofe of this power of God, and of the diuinity of Chrift our Lord, and the vnfpeakable bounty of the *Holy Ghoft* was the fo fpeedy illuminating, & inflaming the foule of this *Baron*. Who, as foone as he receaued the notice of his death, did, in his proportion, follow the example of the *Bleffed Apoftle*. For as he, to Chrift our Lord, appearing fayd, *O Lord, what wilt thou haue me doe*; fo did this noble Caualliere of Chrift, when

when the Preift, & Lieutenant of God fpake to him,
giue himfelfe away by thefe
words, as the *Relation* sheweth; *Do* (y) *you, in the place of*

(y) The
inftant
quiet re-
fignatiõ
of this
Baron
to the
goodwil
of God.

God commaund me, I giue my
felfe, as bound into your hands;
and further it affirmeth,
that he fuffered himfelfe to
be managed, as if he had
beene made, of the foftest
waxe.

It is not impoffible for
a man to meete with fome
Roaring Boy, who may
thinke that the *Baron* was
to fubmiffe. But it is one
thing

thing to be a Roarer of the damned Crue, and another to be an humble member of the body of Chriſt; who aſſured vs, by his owne ſacred mouth, *That* (z) *vnleſſe we became as children, we ſhould neuer enter into the kingdome of heauen* . The world was loſt by the *pride*, and preſumption of the firſt *Adam*; & repaired by the *humility* of the ſecond . And (a) he that conſiders well, how greate that *Humility* was ; and whoſe it was ; and for whoſe ſake, and at the will of

(z) Humility is the true badge, of true Chriſtianity.

(a) The incomparable humility of Ieſus Chriſt our Lord.

of whom , he exercised the
same ; had need of a great
proportion of stupidity , to
make him thinke , that,
since God himselfe vouch-
safed to be at the command
of those base and impure
wretches , who tooke of his
cloathes, and required him
to submit himselfe to those
scourges , those thornes ,
those nayles, those blasphe-
mies , for our sakes , and
sinnes ; yet , on the other
side, this (b) man, this proud
rebellious worme , this
crumme of dust , this drop
of

(b) An
vgly and
abhomi-
nable
pre-
sumpti-
on.

of filth; might keep, for-
footh, a kind of State, and
should not rather fubmit
himfelfe (in imitation of
the humility of Chrift our
Lord) not only to Superi-
ours, but to equalls, and e-
uen inferiours alfo, and in
fine to al (c) the world when
iuft occafion should be offered.

The foule of this noble
Man, was fo well foftned, &
fweetned, by the vnction of
the Holy Ghoft; as that
neither the greatnes of his
Nobility, nor the ardour of

his

(c) This
is the
aduice
of S.
Peter;
*Subditi
eftote
omni
creatu-*

his youth, nor the naturall
boyling courage of his hart,
nor the fresh memory of
his prosperity, nor the vn-
expected arriual of his misery, could make (d) him
once repine, or keep him
from instantly abasing himselfe. But falling deeply v-
pon the consideratiō of his
sinnes; and weighing duely
how full of demerit he was,
in the sight of God; and
knowing exactly, that no-
thing is so truly ignoble,
as a soule which hath for-
feited his grace; and that

rich

(d) A
hart
which is
truely
touched
by Gods
holy spi-
rit, will
ouer-
come
strange
difficul-
tyes.

rich, or *poore*, is little to the purpose ; but (e) that the thing which imports, is to be, or not to be, the feruant, or fonne of God ; it is not ftrange, to fee him caft himfelfe at the feet of common foldiars ; and to ftretch out his hands, with fuch meeknes, at the will of the meaneft Iaylours, for the loue of our Lord, to fignify therby the deteftation wherein he had himfelfe, for hauing fo prefumptuoufly offended, that *Eternall Maiefty*, which by all the Angells is

(e) wherin eternal, true Nobility doth confift.

C   ado-

adored.

(f) The reasons why he was so frequent in confessing his sins.

From (f) hence also did it proceed, that he so frequently confessed himselfe, in that last night of his life; & could neuer thinke that he had sufficiétly deplored his errours, and detested the discorrespondence, and ingratitude, wherewith he had answered, the vnspeakable benefits, of Almighty God. Wherein if any man should thinke, that he did vse excesse; it willbe much more lawfull for me to doubt, that himselfe, either

hath

hath a meane conceit of the *Infinite Maiesty* which is offended; or an ignorant apprehension, of the deformity of al sinne which is committed; or a proud, & paltry mistaking, of the *Nothing* which man was, till he was created; and the worse then *Nothing*, which afterward he grew, by sinning. For (g) he that põders these particulers, as he ought; and knoweth, that the offeces into which he falleth are innumerable; and that the least of them, which is

(g) If you weigh these thinges wel, you will change your wondring at him, into wondring at your selfe.

C 2   com-

committed against an *infinit Maiesty* , in respect of the obiect , is also infinite ; and that , as no one good deed shalbe vnrewarded, by the rich Mercy of God , in Christ our Lord ; so no one trãsgression shal be left vnpunished , by his exquisite Iustice ; wil easily belieue, that in the space of a night , it is hard for one to be too curious , & too carefull , in setting straight the accoũt of his whole life , vnder the piercing eye of Almighty God . But this *Baron* , did,

even

euen by moments, in that short tyme which was left, by the goodnes of God, acquire new (h) light, & gaine new loue of our Lord, and new contempt, & detestation of himselfe; and in the strength thereof, he found some actions to confesse, which he had not conceaued to be sinnes before; & others which he had confessed, he had confessed with a sorrow, far inferiour, to that which then he felt.

(h) Great light of God is wont to breed greate loue of him, & greate sorrow, for hauing so shamefully offended him.

For abstracting from the consideration which he

C 3   had

had of his finnes, againft
God (in refpecte whereof,
no foule is fufficiently able
to quake, and tremble vn-
der him) I truft there is not
a readers eye in the world fo
dimme, as not to difcerne
his vndaunted hart . And
(i) that , no thought of
death, had any power, to
take the leaft clarity from
his vnderftandinge ; the
leaft prefence from his memory; the leaft agility from
his witte ; the leaft order
from his fpeach; or fo much
as the leaft *puntillio*, from
the

(i) The vndaun-ted cou-rage of this Ba-ron .

the ciuill refpects and com-
plementes, which are vfed
amongft perfons of his Nation, and Condition. Nor
yet, on the other fide, shall
any man haue reafon to
thinke, that the punctuali-
ty, which (throughout the
proceffe of this *Relation*) he
shall find to haue been obferued by the *Baron*, in this
laft (k) kind of courtefy, did (k) This
proceed from the leaft affe- courtefy
ctation thereof. Perhaps, & com-
plement
if we looke neere home, we was not
affected,
may find fome example to but free
and na-
haue been giuen of this, not turall.

C 4   long

longe agoe ; but in the prefent cafe , no fufpition of it, can be intertained;both for many other reafons, which will occurre to him that readeth the *Relation* ; and becaufe (as I fayd before) thefe exact tearmes of Honour , and other refpects to the company,which then is prefent, are is it were naturall to men of his country, and quality ; and there would coft them more paines , to omit them (vnleffe their mindes were put into diforder , by fome paffion) then

then it would coſt others,
to obſerue them, where they
were not ſo naturall, as being learnt by induſtry, and
art . But yet, that in ſo ſad
a caſe, this man, would,
for good manners, forbeare
to ſet vp his leggs; or would
not ſo much, as ſtretch himſelfe in the ſight of others,
though his body did much
incline him to it (according
to that mention which the
Relation makes therof) may
wel go for a great argument
in him, of ciuility, of mo-
deſty, and of magnanimity.

C 5   And

And this is that which I thought fit to repreſent to you, by way of *Preface*, to this *Story*. You will find the traces & foot-ſteps of putting men to death, and of the proceedinge which is held with (i) delinquents, to be very different, from that of our Countrey, both concerning the body, and the ſoule. I take not vpon me, to ſay which are better, and which are worſe. With vs, the *Proceſſe* of criminall perſons, is euer made, in the face of the world; but they

are

are not fuffered to haue any
aduocates who may defend
their caufes . In moſt other
Countryes, the delinquéts
are permitted to haue Ad-
uocates , but the *Proceſſe* is
made , though in publique
Court, yet only in prefence
of the Iudges and fome few
Aduocates, and Officers .
With vs,the delinquéts are
fuffered to liue fome dayes
after their comdemnation ;
which certainely is meant
in compaſſion to them ; in
other parts , after they are
iudged to dye,and that fo it

is

is declared , they thinke
they do men a greater courtefy, in putting them quickly out of paine. With vs ,
there is no difference in the
manner of death , between
a Clowne, & the beſt Gen-
tleman of the Kingdome,
vnder the degree of a *Baron*,
vnleſſe it be , in ſome very
rare caſe , by moſt particuler fauour of his *Maieſty*; but
in all other places, that I
haue ſeene , all Gentlemen
are beheaded, to diſtinguiſh
them , frō ſuch as are ignoble. With vs , no indignity

is

is euer done to a *Noble man*
of (m) *Title*, by binding of (m) fuch
his hands, or armes, or the as Barôs
like ; and that cuftôme I them.
commend, as full of Ho-
nour ; but in many other
places, they beare no fuch
refpects ; in regard of the
experiéce which they haue
found, and ẛ feare, which
ftill they are in, of infolen-
cies.

    But for as much, as
concernes the comfort of
criminalls, in the preparation of their foules, towards
the death of their bodyes,
                I can-

I cannot but note it, as a point of charity, and piety most (n) remarkeable, that in very many of the good townes of *Italy* and *Spayne*, there are certain *Companies*, or *Confraternities*, of Gentlemen, well borne and bred; who put this obligation of duty vpon themselues, to visit the prisons, especially in the night precedent to any executiõ. And, togeather with Religious persons, and Ghostly Fathers, they watch, and pray, and exhort, and comfort the

(n) It is the grea-test cha-rity, to help mē to dye well.

the poorest criminalls of
the Country, with the same
industry, & charity, which
is heere, affoarded to this
Noble man. And they ac-
company them all, to their
death; and sometimes, they
discharge their dying harts
of care ; either by vnder-
taking to pay some of their
debtes, or by assisting the
poore wife, and children,
which are left behind ; or
by obliging themselues, to
get (o) *Masses* celebrated for
their soules. And in con-
formity of these good en-
deauours,

(o) S. Monica vpō the point of her death, desired S. Augustine her Sonne, that he would pray for her soule at the altar, whē she should be dead, and so he did. *Vide Augustᵒ Confesˡᵒ l. 9. cap. 11, & 13.*

deauours, we see men dye in those partes, with another manner of disposition towardes God, then vsually they haue with vs. Where it is a lamentable thing, to see many of so profane stupidity, that after liues most lewdly lead, they go either drunke, or dauncing tothe gallowes. As if, they were but to dye in a play; or as if, after this life, there were no immortality of the soule; or els, at least, no account to be rendred, I say not, of idle words (which yet must

be

be done) but of most wicked deeds, wherof many of
them are guilty.

The example which
heere we haue in hand, will
read, to all the Readers of it
in generall, a good lesson
of humility, patience, courtesy, magnanimity, obedi-
ence, and charity. And (p)
it may serue for an instruction, not only to such as
dye, by the hand of human
Iustice; but to al them also,
who are to dye by the hand
of God, as we al shalbe sure
inough to do. That so, we

(p) All
kind of
people
may
profit,
by the
good
lessons
which
are heer
deliue-
red.

D   may

may the better take heede
of finne, which is to be fo
bitterly bewayled; and the
more deeply we be fallen
into it, the more inftantly
we muft implore the mer-
cy, & goodnes of Almigh-
ty God; and difpofe our
felues to the doing of pennance; that fo, by his fauour, we may fecure our
foules, from the danger of
being plunged, into that
lake of eternall paine. This
leffon I fay, may reach to al
Readers in generall. But
particuler Readers may
take

take out particuler leſſons for themſelues. The *Mother* will bid Mothers be inceſſantely carefull for their children; the *Sonne* wil coniure men from being inſolent, or diſobedient towards their parentes; and the (q) *Confortatori* wil exhort them to shew all charity to their diſtreſſed neighbours. And I beſeech our Lord Ieſus, to graunt ſuch graces both to them and me, as his diuine Maieſty knoweth to be moſt needfull for vs.

(q) Theſe are they who comfort the deliquents in their death.

D2 THE

THE DEATH
OF THE MOST
ILLVSTRIOVS
LORD, SIGNOR
TROILO SAVELLI,

Who was beheaded in *Rome*, in
the Caſtle of *Sant Angelo*, on
the 18. of Aprill 1592.

T H E Writing
of the liues or
deaths of o-
thers, if they
be full of ex-
traordinary accidents, doe

vſu-

vſually make the Readers
wonder; if they be dolorous
they cauſe compaſſion ; if
proſperous, men grow therby into a deſire ; if aduerſe,
into a feare. But this death,
which now I am going a-
bout to deliuer, doth ſo im-
brace the accidents of all
theſe kinds; that whoſoeuer
shall read it, as he ought,
will (ᵃ) eaſily perceaue, his
mind to be al filled at once,
with al thoſe affectiõs . And
althogh, that which I write,
be, in fine, no more then a
meere *Relation* of a mans
Death,

(a) The
power
which
this diſ-
courſe,
wil haue
ouer
many
affecti-
ons, all
at once .

Death, yet perhaps it may ferue for a guide and example of men, through the whole courfe of their life.

I will nakedly therfore, declare the progreffe, and period of this accident; as in the night, when it happened, I went obferuing it pace by pace, to the comfort of myne owne foule. For (b) heere, all affectation, and ornament of fpeach, would but profane the majefty of the thing; and no indeauour, or ftrife of wit, would euer arriue to the ex-

D 4   preffi-

(b) This *Relation* is purpofely written, in a naturall,& plaine manner.

preſſion thereof . I will direct it only to them , who
if perhaps they haue not
perſonall and proper ex-
perience, of the admirable
effects of Gods grace ; at
leaſt they will eyther haue
belieued them of others,
or reade of them in good
books, or heard them often
deliuered by preachers. For,
as for ſuch, as are meer ſträ-
gers therunto, theſe things
to them will ſeeme incredible . Though euen by ſuch,
they may yet be thought
the more probable, when
at

at length they shall vnderftand; that at the inftance
of his excellent Mother,
one of the Fathers (c) of the
Chiefa noua, had, with moft
diligent, and deuout cha-
rity, exercifed his life, for
the fpace of a moneth, in
fpirituall thinges, whofe
death I haue vndertaken to
defcribe; and whatfoeuer
effect it may haue, more
or leffe, I will be fure to
write it for the benefit of
foules, and vpon no other
motiue.

(c) Thefe
are the
good
Prieftes
of the
Oratory
which
was in-
ftituted
by that
greate
feruant
of God,
*B. Phi-
lippus
Nereus.*

It was then, vpon the
D 5   17. of

17. of Aprill at (d) foure houres of the night, of that fryday; when the newes was brought, to the Lord *Troilo Sauelli* of his Death, by an inferiour Officer. Who coming to that chamber, where the Noble man was at his reſt, ſayd to him in this manner: Your Lordſhip may be pleaſed to riſe, and apparaile your ſelfe. Whereunto he anſwered; *This indeed is an houre, which hath a little of the vnſeaſonable; but yet whither wilt thou conduct me?* The fellow tould him,

(d) This might be about eleuen of the clocke at night, after our account.

him, That place was to be made for new prisoners; so deuising this excuse, that he might not fright him all at once. *I beleeue* (saith the young Lord) *what thou hast told me; but I confesse, thou madest me halfe afrayde;* and then, sittinge vp in his bed, he said, *Let vs apparaile our selfe, in the name of* God.

Hauing begun to put on his cloathes, and as he was descending from his bed, *Giue me leaue,* saith he, *for so long, as that I may be ready.* And so, casting an earnest

earneſt countenance towardes a little Picture of our B·*Lady*, with *Chriſt* in her armes (which there he had of purpoſe) he recommended himſelfe in great earneſt, as afterward he related to me. And the ſame night (ſome houre before the arriuall of this newes) he had raiſed himſelfe out of his bed; and (kneeling downe before that (e) Picture) he ſayd, with abundant teares, *O bleſſed and glorious Virgin, O that I might dye, yf dye I muſt, with this very diſpoſition,*

which

(e) He prayed before the picture, but he prayed to the B. Virgin to pray for him; and he thought it no ill way to go by the Mother to the Son, as the Fathers, & Saints of Gods Church had don before him.

which now I find in my hart.
He told me, that the fame
night, when firſt he went
to bed, he did, in a manner,
aſſure himſelfe that he was
to haue had his life ſaued;
but that yet, more ſuddainly then he euer vſed, he
roſe vp, and could not hold
from diſcharging his hart
towardes the *Bleſſed Virgin.*
This was an ordinary vſe
of his., as afterward thoſe
ſouldiers, vnder whoſe cuſtody he was, related to me;
for they often feigning not
to ſee him, did many times
per-

perceaue , that by ſtealth
he caſt himſelfe, vpon his
knees .

As ſoone as he was
apparailed , the Officer returning , and doubting ,
leaſt (by reaſon of his freſh
youth , being encountred
with ſuch a terrible , and
ſuddaine accidét) he might,
through a kind of deſpaire-
full rage , either do hurt to
himſelfe , or elſe to others ,
would needs, vpon a ſud-
daine , caſt the manicles
vpon his hands; but gently
ſtretching them out ; *My*
friend

friend, (f) *sayth he, behould,*
I am heere, ready to obey thy
will, and the will of all the
world, since the will of God is
such. Hauing manicled him,
they (g) lead him towardes
the Chappell; when, at the
issue out of his chamber, he
blessed (h) himself, the best
he could with the signe of
the holy *Crosse,* with both
his hands.; and casting vp
his eyes to heauen, he profoundly sighed .For, seeing
perhappes, that there was
more

(f) The earely, & humble resignation of this Noble man.

(g) By this time others were come in.

(h) He armed himselfe with the signe of the holy Crosse - *Ad omnem actum, ad omnem*

necessum manus pingat Crucem: At euery action, and
in euery motion let thy hand make the signe of the
Crosse, D , *Hier. epist. ad Eustoch, 22. cap. 16.*

more people, then might
be needful for the changing
of his lodging, *This*, sayth
he, *is another manner of busines,
then to change me only, from one
place to another; but by the grace
of God, I am ready for all.*

Thus, silently going
downe to the Chappell, he
was mett by the (1) *Gouernour*, & the *Proueditore*, and
by three others of them,
who are called *Confortatori
della misericordia*, in a fashiõ,
very sutable to the occasion. Then one of them sayd
to

(i) There
are Con-
gregati-
ons of
Gen-
tlemen
in Rome
(as there
are also
in other
great
Cittyes
of Italy
& Spay-
ne) who
imploy
them-
selues
for the
helping
of con-
demned
men, to
dye wel.
The *Go-
uernour
and Pro-*
ueditore are chiefe officers of these Congregations.

to him in this manner : My „
Lord, the houre which God „
hath prefixed for you, is e- „
uen run out ; render your „
felfe into his mercifull han- „
des. And he, without be-
ing troubled, otherwife,
then by fetching a fighe
(which yet was both foft, &
fhort) did anfwere thus;
Let God be bleffed; behold I ren-
der my felfe to him ; and difpofe
you of me. And fo thofe good
and charitable Brothers of
that *Congregation*, with fome
Fathers of the *Society of Ie-*
fus, cafting thefelues round

E   about

about him; and endeauou-
ring to sweeten the bitternes of that newes, by dif-
creet & decent meanes, did
comfort him the best they
could. He yielded to all,
& did euen preuent them;
& then, knocking his brest,
and bowing down his head,
and kissing the *Crucifixe*, he
demanded pardon, and like
gentle waxe, did suffer himselfe to be managed by them
all.

One of those *Conforta-
tori*, did, before all other
thinges, put him in mind
of

of making his *Confession*. V-
pon the very firſt naming
whereof (recollecting himſelfe) he ſayd, *And (*k*) where
is the Confeſſour?* And they
ſhewing him a Prieſt of
their Company , with his
Albe (l) vpon his backe, and
his *Stole* about his necke
(that afterward he might
ſay Maſſe, in the proper
tyme)the firſt thing he did,
was to be confeſſed ; and we
all went out, to leaue the
place free to them .

He being confeſſed, and
we returned, we began to
E 2   diſ-

(k) The firſt thing he did, was to confeſſe himſelf.

(l) Theſe are ſome of the ſacerdotall veſtmentes which are vſed in the celebrating of Maſſe.

difpofe him, towards a good
end, by diuers fpiritual ex-
ercifes, fit for that purpofe.
And after many had fpoké,
I alfo beganne thus to fay;
« *Signor Troilo*, This is that
« paffage, which whofoeuer
« doth once make well, doth
« acquire eternall felicity; &
« if once it be ill made, it
« draweth after it, an euerla-
« fting mifery. It now imports
« your Lordship to make it
« well, that you may efcape
« that eternity of torment.
« This paffage is narrow, vn-
« euen, hard, & full of ftones,
                                            and

and thornes; all the world
doth see it, and your Lordship finds it by experience;
but (m) behold sweet Iesus,
who, by his goodnes, will
euen it all. Cast your selfe,
my Lord, vpon him; and
then you will be able to say
with courage, *Omnia* (n) *pos-*
sum, in eo qui me confortat.

  He answered thus, with
a cheerefull, and euen smiling coūtenance, *Omnia pos-*
sum in eo qui me comfortat. By
the mercy of my deere Iesus, I
know the necessity of making this
passage well; I acknowledge his

(m) Our
Lord
Iesus,
doth e-
uen, the
vneuen
way of
death.

(n) I
can do al
thinges
in him
that
cōforts
me.

pro-

prouidence ouer me, and to his prouidence I add, that, of his loue. For as much as with extraordinary loue it is, that he hath brought me hither. I see it, I cõfesse it. And how often, deere Father, haue I beene, as I may say, in the very iawes of death; which if at that tyme it had seized vpon me, infallibly this soule, and body of myne had perished. Behold (o) *the cunning of my Christ; to saue me, he hath made choyce of this way.* And then bowing, & baring his head, and with great life of spirit, rayfing himfelf from his

(o) He acknowledgeth, and accepteth of Gods prouidence, with great alacrity.

his chayre, he further added; *I accept of this election, which God hath made;* & then casting himselfe vpon his knees, before the *Altar, Nay I thanke thee* (sayth he) *O my good Father, for thy so faythfull, and louing care of me; who haue not only beene a wandring, but a contumacious Sonne of thyne. To thee it doth belong, to smooth and euen the ruggednes of this way; since thou hast been pleased to addresse me by it.* And so, bowing his face euen almost downe to the ground, he remayned a

E 4   while,

while, in mentall Prayer.

Being therfore wished to fit downe, he was fcarce fetled in that pofture, when turning towardes me, he fayd thus, in myne eare : *You, whom through my good fortune, I haue heere, to help me, in this fo weighty and high affayre, in the place of God do yow commaund me. I* (p)*giue my felfe, as bound into your hands. The Prince hath difpofed of my body; do you as much with my foule.* I fayd therfore to him : I firft defyre, my Lord, that you make the

pro.

(p) He giueth himfelfe away to his Ghoftly Father.

proteftation (q) which is wont
to be beliuered by fuch as
are going to God. Which
being publikely pronoun-
ced by him, with great fenfe
and fpirit, (he taking vp
& repeating my wordes) I
aduifed him further thus:
Yow shall now make all
thofe actes of Contrition,
which I shall call to your
mind; hauing the eyes therof , firft bent vpon God,
being offended, as a *Crea-*
tour , as a *Preferuer* , as a
Iuftifier , and as a *Glorifier* .
Next, vpon your felfe, who

(q) This is a decla ration of his fayth with an entiere fubmiffion to the good will of God.

E 5   haue "

,, haue offended him ; being
,, his creature , his houſehold
,, ſeruant, his Chriſtian ſlaue;
,, and one ſo deeply obliged ,
by his benefits . Thirdly ,
vpon the offences themſelues which you haue com-
mitted ; and be ſory at your
hart, for hauing committed
them ; and (r) if not in particuler for them all, at leaſt
for the (s) moſt greiuous of
them, which ſhall repreſent
theſelues to your memory .
Fourthly , vpon the good
which you haue omitted; &
the tyme which you haue
loſt

(r) For who can euer call to mind all his particuler ſins .

(h) He had already confeſ-ſed his ſinns; & now he is but exhor-ted to renew his ſor-row for them.

loſt ; and the yeares that „
you haue miſpent . Fiftly , „
vpon the ſcandall which „
you haue giuen . And if any „
thing more be to be done ; „
if (:) to make reſtitution , (t) **We**
eyther of fame , or goods ; cannot
if to pardon others , or to be ſaued
aſke pardon your ſelf; reſto- vnles
re , and pardon , and aſke firſt we
pardon . If to perfourme make
any vowes , or fulfill any reſtituti-
promiſes , performe , and on, as
fullfill them . Or finally , if well of
you leaue any debts , or if fame, as
you will make any ſignifi- of goods
cation of your repentance , if it lye
             and „ in our power

„ and pious end, you are now
„ to put your hand to worke.

To thefe thinges he offered himfelfe moft readily ; and did execute them all , with fo great deuotion , that euery one now began , to change his ftyle, in fpeaking to him . And finding , that whereas before , they thought they should haue to do but with a yong man , or rather but with a youth , and weakeling , (u) they

(u) He infinitly ouercame their expectatiō.

were now to treate , with a manly , generous , and ripe Chriftian (far fuperiour to that

that , which might perad-
uenture haue been expected
of him) one of the *Confortatori* , began with greate
difcretion, to difcourfe vpon the horrour of Death ,
which our moft fweete
Chrift Iefus , did by his
agony difpoffeffe of bitternes . Confide , faith he , and ,,
caft your thoughts vpon ,,
him, and fay, *Pone(* x *) me Do-*
mine iuxta te, & cuiufuis manus
pugnet contra me . And if now
you find any bitter taft in
death in this short night ,
as without fayle you will ,
                        fay ,

(x) Place
me, O
Lord ,
neere to
thee, &
let the
hand of
any o.
ther
fight a-
gainft
me.

(v) O
my Fa-
ther, not
as I will,
but as
thou wilt
thy will
be done.

say, *Pater* (y) *mi , non sicut ego
volo , sed sicut tu , fiat voluntas
tua.*

The contrite Lord ,
made answere thus , *The
wickednes of my life doth fright
me , more, then the bitternes of
my death. O how wrechedly haue
I spent these eighteene yeares ?
How ill haue I vnderstood my
Sauiour? How vngratefull haue
I beene for his noble fauours ?
How rebelliously haue I liued
against his lawes? And now
haue I run like a wild, vnbridled
horse , in these later yeares of
mine ; without any manner of
restraint*

restraint, wheresoeuer the pre-
sent occasions, or conuersations,
or (z) rather (for I haue sayd
ill) wheresoeuer myne owne pas-
sions, and blind affections, had a
mind to plunge me? It is I, and
none but I, who did precipitate
me; and yet you bid me fixe my
thoughts, and hopes vpon God;
and say, Pone me Domine iuxta
te, & cuiusuis manus pugnet
contra me, fiat voluntas tua.

(z) The
sinner, is
only to
blame
himselfe
for ha-
uing sin-
ned.

Vpon this, another of
the *Confortatori*, did thus „
proceed. It is an acte of „
magnanimity, not to feare „
the angry face of death; & „

of

„ of humility, to acknowledg
„ our offences; but of confi-
„ dence, to hope for pardon,
„ as your Lordship doth ;
„ who well may fay, *Propter*
„ *nomē tuum Domine, propitiabe-*
ris peccato meo, multum eſt enim.
For thy names ſake O Lord
thou shalt forgiue my ſin,
for it is great. *O how great,*
ſayd *Signor Troilo? Euen as*
greate, after a manner, as is
the mercy of God, which is
immenſe.

The *Proueditore* then
„ ſayd; Your Lordship, may,
„ if you ſo be pleaſed, make
your

your laſt *VVill*, and *Teſtament*; to the end that no o-
ther thought may ſollicite
you, but of your ſoule alon.

Heereupon the *Baron*,
without the leaſt delay, by
way of anſwere, did bid thē
write. And hauing taken
out of his pocket, a little
note, which he carryed a-
bout him, he did ſuddainly
dictate his *Teſtament*; wherin he deliuered ſome particulers, which, in my opinion, are very conſiderable.
Firſt, (a) of tender Deuotiō;
for he recommended his

F   ſoule

(a) The conſiderations which may be made, vpon the manner of penning his will.

ſoule to God, by moſt deare, and religious wordes . Secondly, of Ripenes , which was more then of a young man; becauſe, in a moſt particuler manner , he had remembrance of all his ſeruants . Thirdly, of a moſt liuely Contrition; becauſe, with a moſt profound , internall affection of mind , he demaunded pardon of many, euen by name. Fourthly, of great Magnanimity; becauſe he coniured the Lady his Mother, that ſhe would pardon all his aduerſaryes,

saryes, as he himſelfe did pardon them a thouſand tymes ouer. Beſeeching (b) her, by a long, and chriſtian circuite of wordes, that she would neuer reſent his death; but he layd the fault vpon himſelfe, in al things. Fiftly, of Religious Piety; leauing large almes to many Churches, & other holy places; accommodating many poore (c) Virgins, with dowryes, at the particuler diſcretion, and to be performed by the care of his heyres; that God might

(b) what a true, and noble Chriſtian hart wasthis?

(c) This is a deuotion, and charity, much vſed in Italy.

F 2   the

the rather haue mercy on him. Sixtly, of entiere Iuſtice; becauſe he tooke care, that euen more then was due by him, should be reſtored. Seauenthly, of noble Gratitude; becauſe he rewarded, whoſoeuer had done him any ſeruice in priſon. Eightly, of affectuous Reuerence; becauſe he did in a moſt ſweet, and deere manner, aske pardon, of the Lady his Mother, & of the reſt of his kinred, beſids the expreſſing of other complements.

Hauing

Hauing ended his laſt *VVill*, *VVell Syrs* (ſayth he) *behold we haue this reſidue of tyme, now wholy free, for the care of our ſoule.* And turning towards me, he ſayd, *It* (d) *is in your hand, and therefore diſpoſe of it; for this only is now, in my power to giue you.* I then, by way of anſwere ſayd, Giue your ſelfe, my Lord, to IESVS. *I do ſo*, ſayd he; and he ſayd it inſtantly. And I againe, Giue your ſelfe wholy to him. He ſayd, *I do.* Conſecrate your ſelfe; he ſtil ſayd, *I do.*

(d) He ſpeakes of his ſoule, for as much as concerned the guiding of it, vnder God. »
»
»
»
»

F 3   Make

(e) As al grieuous sinners are, if they do not throghly repēt, which no man can be sure that he hath sufficiently done, though he may haue great hope thereof.

(f) A reftament, is not valide there, if it haue not feauen witnesses at the leaſt .

Make your ſelfe, ſayd I, entierely his . *But how (ſayth he) O Father, ſhall I make my ſelfe entierely his, if I be vnworthy, and if perhaps, I be an enemy* (e) *of his* . But in the meane tyme, whileſt the *VVill* was in writing, he that wrote it, put vs in mind, that it was to be publikely read ; that ſo it might be ſhut vp, with a due (f) number of witneſſes . And whyleſt this was in doing, that is, whyleſt the *Notary* was reading of it ; three thinges of

of some consideration did
occurre. The first, that whé
he read how he recommen-
ded his soule to God, *My
body* (sayth he, (drawing
neere me, according to his
custome) *I dispose not of; for
now, it is no longer myne. It
once was myne, and I would it
had not beene so; but* (g) *it is
more thé reason, that I hauing
had so great care of it, in my
life tyme, for my punishment,
should not be suffered, to haue
any power ouer it, now in my
death. Let them therefore doe
with it what they will; for I*

(g) He
acknow-
ledgeth
the pro-
uidence,
and iu-
stice of
God, in
al things

F 4 *Sa-*

sacrifice it to God whatsoeuer it be . Father , will not such an oblation as this , doe me good? It will, said I; without doubt it will ; and what (h) more acceptable oblation, can be made to our Lord , then that of the body? The second, That when the *Legacies* were read ; it being obserued, by the manner of expressing one of them , that he deliuered himselfe as faulty, in a certaine thing, wherein indeed he was not so ; and therefore the *VVill* was to be redressed , as I desi-

(h) For he that giues his body, doth shew in good earnest, that he hath already giuen his soule .

desired, which serued not only, (as before) for securing of his conscience, but for the sauing also of his honour. Vpon this, putting off his *Montiera*, or capp, *O Father*, saith he (and he did it halfe smiling) *are you now taking care of my reputation, and of the puntillios of Honour, and of that smoake or vanity of the world? Let my soule be saued, & let al the vaine Honour perish, which I eyther had, or might haue had . Do you not remember that which euen* (i) *now you sayd*, Mihi

F 5   mun-

(i) This is not mentioned heer before; but he said also many other thinges which are not mentioned in this short *Relatiō*.

(k) The world is crucified to me, and I to it.

mundus (k) crucifixus est, & ego mundo. *In a word, let not the soule be touched, but let my Honour be blasted, according to that accompt, which the blinde world is wont to make of Honour; that it may serue as a part of the punishement, which is due to me.* The third, that at the same instant, his hat was brought him; and one of his people, being desirous to take his *Montiera* from off his head, *what are you doing* sayth he? They answered, they would giue him his hat. But he bad them

them let it alone , saying,
That it imported not ; and he
added , with a soft voyce,
Looke heer a whyle; they would
faine honour this head of mine ,
which I am to loose , within
few houres , for my sinnes .

The *Will* being then
read , and shut; he throwing himselfe , as it were
vpon me , with a most mo-
dest kind of sweetnes , said,
Father I am already reconciled;
but I would faine make a gene-
rall Confession of my whole life,
to your Reuerence. And althogh,
since I came into prison , I did

the

the same, in effect, at the instan-
ce of my Lady, my Mother;
yet know, that I had then no
light, or feeling of my sinnes,
in respect of that, which now I
discouer in my hart. For, One
thing it is, deare Father, for a
man to confesse himselfe, when
he is in the sight of death; and
another, to do it not thinking of
death; or at least, but conside-
ring it, as a far off. And so,
calling for a (l) little booke,
which he had aboue in the
prison (shewing a man the
way, how to confesse his
sinnes, exactly well (which

his

(l) There
are eue-
ry wher
to be
had litle
bookes,
of ad-
dresse,
wherby
men are
taught
how to
confesse
their sins
exactly.

his good MOTHER had
brought to him some dayes
before) he began his *confes-*
fion. Wherin, my Lord God
doth knowe, that, as it is
lawfull for me, by that moſt
ample authority, which
himſelf gaue me, to declare
as much therof, as I should
thinke fit; ſo if I were able
to expreſſe it, I ſay not, that
Rome would be aſtonished
at it, but all *Italy* would be
ſo . For if I ſpeake of the
exact manner that he held;
for as much as concerned
the particuler deſcending
euen

(m) *Confession* is no such cursory or superficiall thing, as they which know it not, conceaue, & say.

euen to idle wordes , and anie other (m) such little thing , me thought I was hearing some well exercised Religious man . In the explicating of circumstances, and the vnfolding of intricate and intangled cases, it was , as if he had bin some profound Deuine. In relating the determinate number, & the various kindes of his sins; he made proofe of one , who had a most fresh, and happy memory.

This rare Gentleman pawsing now and then , betweene

tweene the Confeſſion of
his ſinnes ; and ſuffering
certaine teares to fall qui-
etly vpon my knees , he
would be wiping them
away ; and that being done,
he would often vſe to ſay
with ſighes; *O Father* , *how* (n) (n) He
good hath our Lord been to me ?   had
Let him now be bleſſed , *as often* , great
and yet more often , *then I haue*   reaſon
offended him , *in my former life* .   to ſay ſo.
Whyleſt he was accuſing
himſelfe of his faults , he
would expreſſe thé , in certaine few, but they, all liuely, ánd moſt pious wordes;
                    and,

(o) He pawled sometymes between both to rest himselfe, & to recall his sins, more freshly to his memory; for though it were interrupted, it was al but one *Confessiõ* till the *Absolution* were giuen.

(p) An admirable Contrition.

and in som particuler cases, so dearely tender; that, in his countenance, one might see euident signes, of how his very hart, was euen rent, within. So that between (o) the times of his *confessiõ*, the *Confortatori*, (doubting least perhaps he might grow to faint) would be asking him if he needed not somewhat to restore, & comfort himself. To which he answered (speaking priuatly, & more then once to me) *This* (p) *only comfort, or restoratiue I would*

would defire; That my very hart
might burft for griefe; and fa-
tisfaction might fo be (q) giuen,
for my finnes, if perhaps euen
that, would ferue the turne.

But for as much as, to
my thincking, he did melt
as it were by fo enlardging
himfelfe in his *Confeffion*,
had an eye vpon him, and I
ventured to fay thus vnto
him. My deare *Signor Troi-*
lo, be not fo exceffiuely cu- "
rious, and particuler, in "
accufing your felfe; efpeci "
ally of thofe your former "
finnes, which lye not now "

G   vpon "

(q) To the iuftice of God; his forrow being dignified by the death & paffion, of Iefus Chrift, our Lord.

(r) See
how
truely
this hart
was tou-
ched
with for-
row for
his fins;
and the
know-
ledge of
himfelf.

vpon your foule. O (r) *Father* (fayd he) *I haue wafted my whole life, in offending God; and will you haue me, or shall I content my felfe, in one fingle houre, to demaund pardon of fo many offences? So long in finning, and fo short in confeffing my finnes? That I am troublefome to you, my deare Father, I well difcouer; but what can I doe withall, if I be forced to it?* And heer againe, he began to make for himfelfe, a very bath of teares. And inter-pretinge what I had faid, after his owne conceite,

                                        he

he added , with teares re-
doubled , *And this alſo do my
ſinnes deſerue, by way of pu-
niſhment , that hauing caſt ſo
much, and ſo much time away ,
in preiudice of my ſaluation, I
ſhould now want time , wherein
I might euen confeſſe my ſinnes .*
*Pardon me , deare Father , and
endure this trouble for the loue
of God; for you ſhall* (s) *merit ,
in his ſight, by helping this poore
ſoule of mine, towards ſaluation;
& I will remaine with obligation to you, when I shall go by the
mercy of God & your good meanes, into the place of reſt .* And

(s) To
do a
good
workė
by the
grace,&
for the
loue of
God; is
merito-
rious;
for ſo
Chriſt
our
Lord
hath
made it.

G 2   finding

finding that still he grew in teares, I confesse my weaknes, for I was not able to containe my selfe, from expressing also tendernes, by teares.

As soone as he perceaued this, he said; *Father, your Reuerence weepes, and yet you weepe not for your selfe, but for me; and yet you will not haue me weepe, for my selfe.* But then, both of vs being silent for a time, he after, began againe to confesse, with those accustomed short words, but full of substance, and

and propriety; making me
write down al those things,
which he confided to me,
for the dischardge of his
conscience. Whilest I was
writinge, he would needes
for his contentment hold
the Standish, in his owne
hands; and read those lines,
when I had done; and kisse
them, and then bath them
in teares.

But of nothing did he
accuse himselfe so much, as
of all that, which had any
relation to the Lady, his
Mother. Nor am I able by
G 3 any

any meanes to expresse, with what aboundance of teares, he accompanied those accusations of himselfe. For, beginning euen from his very Infancy,

(t) A lardge expressi-on of the vnspea-kable greife he had, for his diso-bediéce and in-gratitu-de to the Lady his mother.

Father (sayth he) I (t) haue committed many offences against God; yet at this tyme, me thinks, I am not so much afflicted for any thing, as for not hauing knowne, how to serue my selfe, of that tender loue, and pru-dence, and patience, which my Lady my Mother, expressed, in the education of me. For euen when I was yet a child, she gaue me

*me in charge, to certaine learned
and religious Preceptours; who
till I arriued to haue sixteene
yeares of age, did with great fi-
delity, and sufficiency, teach me,
not only the litterature of* Humanity, *but* Philosophy *also.
And so did they further shew,
how I was to addresse my selfe
towardes piety, by their good
example, and aduice. Nor yet
content with this; how sollici-
tous was she also, to procure by
many other meanes, that I might
proceed, both in* Learning, *and*
Vertue? *For* (u) *concerning
that of* Learning, *she gaue me*

(u) See
heer the
Image,
of a holy
and ten-
der-har-
ted mo-
ther

G 4   *Store*

store of *bookes*, of *tyme*, of *oportunity*, and a thousand tender fauours she did me, which were conuenient for those yeares of myne. And for the inducing me to Vertue, she addressed me to choyce of good *Conuersations*, spirituall *Discourses*, excellent *Sermons*, and *Persons*, who might from tyme to tyme giue me counsaile. Commanding me, and causing me to be lead to Confession ; not only vpon all the principall *Feastes* of the yeare, but once moreouer euery moneth.

And, till this very tyme,
when

when I am *speaking* to your Reuerence, you may, if you will
take the paynes, find among my
papers, most euident testimonyes
of what now I am saying; and
especially (x) a short manner of
Instruction, how to spend the
whole day, well. The thinges
besides whereof she did admonish
me, were in a manner, infinite.
VVhen I was yet a little one, she
kept me in bridle, by threates,
yea and by stroakes sometymes;
and when I was growne elder,
she endeauoured to do it, by the
faire meanes, of requests, and
promises; and oftentymes, with

(x) Note
the dili-
gences
which
this holy
mother
did vse,
for the
pious
educati-
on of
her son-
ne.

G 5   *so*

so many teares , as that now, they are as many launces to passe through my hart . For this, did she procure that (y) *blessed man* Philippo, *of the* Chiesa noua *to assiste , and hold me, when I was* confirmed ; *and that afward I should make particuler friendship with him.*

She kept me far off from looking vpon ill examples ; and held me neere her selfe , after the manner , as I may say, of a Religious life ; exhorting me often, day and night, that I would liue

No-

Nobly, (z) *and like a Chriſtian.* (z)True Chriſtia-

Nor did that bleſſed mouth of nity, is true No-

hers, euer ceaſe to ſay, Troi- bility.

lo, my Sonne, feare God, &

loue God . *For this did she*

take vpon her, the gouernement

of all my (a) Caſtles ; *and the* (a) Ca-

care of all my affaires ; liuing Italian,

in a continuall ſtate, of between doth ſig-

hope, and feare, of the proofe both the

that I would made . Nor was houſe,

there a Religious Houſe, *or* and the Towne,

Monaſtery , *to the prayers* or vilage

wherof, she recomended me not . belon-

Nor came there any Religious it.

perſons to her, nor did she meet

with any abroad, to whome, all

forget-

forgettefull of her selfe, she

(b) Som
body
prayed
fo well
for him,
as to
make
him a
Saint.

would not say, Pray (b) *for
my Sonne.*

*And I, vngratefull to her
so great labours, when I grew
to haue sixteene yeares of age,
did render her, so ill payment,
for such a huge summe of loue; as
that I euen parted house with
her; & did outrage her, both by
wordes, and deeds; in such sort,
as that the vttermost of all
punishment, seemeth a hundred
times lesse to me, then my demerit. And when, deare Father,
I thincke vpon the teares with
she was euer sheading for me,*

both

*both by day, and in those nights,
so sadly spent; and on the ago-
nyes which she suffered vpon my
occasion, I find contentment, in
that I am to dye; whereby, me
thinckes, I grow, in part, to
ouershaddowe, so many of my
lewd behauiours.*

*Neither (c) yet, after I had
separated my selfe from her,
did she giue ouer to sollicite me
with notes, and letters, and
messages, and a thousand other
inuentions, that I would be
induced to retire my selfe from
vitious conuersations; and she
wold pray me, & importune me,*

&

(c) The inuinci-
ble loue
of this
Mother,
to her
Sonne.

& coniure me, that I would take to good . And well I know, that no kind of deuotion was omitted by her, for my reformation, both by visiting as many Churches, and Religious persons, as she knew in Rome .

And in fine, she came often to me , both by day and night , whilest I was wandering vp and downe in such company; and (d) when she found me out , she would cast her selfe , euen at my feete , that so I might once be drawen to open mine eyes , and would consider the precipice that I was approaching to ; and the ruines

(d) It seems to haue been a kind of strife & war, be-tweene how kind, a Mother could tel how to be, and how vn-kind a Sonne .

*ruines, besides the shame, that
would ineuitably come vpon me;
and that I would returne to
Christ; and that once, I would
truly weigh (for these were her
very wordes) whose Sonne I
was; and that I would consider,
what thing that was, which euer
had beene wanting to me, that
so, in that desperate fashion, I
should abandone all care of my
Estate, of my Life, and of my
Honour. And vsually she accō-
panyed these admonitions, and
requests of hers, with most tender teares.*

Sometimes againe, she would
turne

turne aside, and casting vp her eyes to God, she would beseech him, either to conuert me, or els (e) to take me to himselfe.

(e) Her prayer was heard in a better, though in another māner, then she most desired.

And this I can say with al truth, that euen from the beginning, to this very houre, wherein now I liue, she hath neuer ceased to procure my saluation. For euen from the first tyme, that she (f) came to see me heere in prison,

(f) She was in Rome at his commitment, but whē she saw

she exhorted me to Confession, and euer since, she hath come, as thicke as haile vpon me, sometymes with Religious men, and some-

how the world would go with him, she retyred frō thence, with her load of sorrow.

*sometymes with pious Books. So
long, that now at last, I am by
the fauour of God, returned a
little into my selfe. And besides
the cutting off, of all occasions of
doing il, she gaue me many great
opportunityes of good ; besides
the exhortations, which she her
selfe made to me, in most feruent
manner, that I would restore
my selfe, to the seruice of God.*

*Nor could euer any Sonne
desire any fauour, or contentment of a Mother, which myne,
did not, of her selfe, impart to
me. And I, on the other side,
haue serued, but to make her life*

H   *most*

most vnfortunate, by this period of myne. I beseech our Lord forgiue me, & to receaue the future affliction of her hart, in present discount of my offences.

Then towardes the end of his Confession ; *I desire* (sayd he) *a fauour of you now, deare Father, which you must not deny me. It is, that I may haue liberty to lament my sinnes* with teares ; *and that, by them, I may giue testimony to the Diuine Maiesty, of the* (g) *griefe, wherewith my harte aboundes within.* Weepe out, sayd I, since our Lord doth giue

you

(g) That so the penitent himselfe by finding it, might haue in-crease of comfort.

you such a desire of wee- "
ping. "

I had scarce brought
forth this last worde, when
allready, there beganne
to fall, a most aboundant
showre of teares from his
eyes; in such sort, (h) as that
he bathed a good part of
one of my armes ; and my
sleeue was as wett through,
as if it had rayned from
aboue. Which accident I
obseruing, after some halfe
quarter of an houre ; and
doubting, least his hart
might so discharg it selfe by

(h) An admirable and almost miraculous Contrition.

H 2   his

his eyes, rather for the apprehension which he might haue of death, then other-
" wise ; I desired, that for
" the loue of *Iesus*, he would
" quiet himselfe, & not mul-
" tiply his affliction, nor con-
" tinue to torment his mind,
in that manner. To this he answered ; *Father, I giue you my fayth, that I do not, at all, bewayle my death ; but I do only, and purely, lament the offences, which I haue committed against Almighty God. And* (i) *I haue so much hope, in the mercy of my deare Lord, that not only*

(i) A happy coniunction of Christiã sorrow, with noble courage.

only I shall shead no teares, for my death; but not so much as change my countenance. Father, I bewayle my most vnfortunate life, and not my most happy death. That life was, indeed, most vnfortunate; whereas this death, is most happy; for in fine, if in that, I liued an enemy to God, I hope, in this, I shall dye his friend.

Well then, sayd I, proceed in your *Confession,* that ,, so you may dye the friend ,, of God; and lay, a part of ,, your tears, aside, the whyle. ,,
Whereupon, the most o-

bedi-

bedient young Gentleman,
accommodatinge himselfe
to my direction , did iuſt
proceed , where he had left.

At this I wondred ſo
much themore; for as much
as I my ſelfe had forgotten
it, though I alſo had one of
thoſe little bookes in my
hand, which inſtruct how a
Confeſſion may be well made.
But he going on , did lay
before me, (as if it had bin
in one ſingle proſpect) the
whole courſe of his life ;
with ſo great clarity , and
breuity , that I found my
                              ſelfe,

felfe , as obliged , to aske him , if during many dayes before , he had not applied himfelfe to make fuch a preparation . To which the yong Noble man made this very anfwere : *So great is the light (as I haue already infinua-ted) which my deare Lord Iefus vouchfafes to giue me at this inftant , of my whole life , that euen whyleft I am confeſſing , me thinkes I behold all my acti-ons* (k) *as in a glaffe ; and I read all my thoughtes, and wordes, as in a booke .*

And, without doubt, H 4 fo

(k) This was a very ex-traordi-nary , fuperna-turall fauour of Al-mighty God.

ſo it was . For he , without euer miſtaking a worde , did ſo call all his ſinnes to minde , that by that time he wanted little of hauing declared them al diſtinctly. Only at the very end , as it were , of his *Confeſſion* , he returned to repeate ſome thinges which he had already ſaid ; and I doubting that he did ſo , as hauing forgotten what he had expreſſed before , I told him of that inaduertence (as I reputed it ,) when yet he made me this anſwere : *I know*

know well, deare Father, that
I repeate some thinges; but I do
it, to the end that I may now
more perfectly detest them, & be
confounded in my selfe. And especially (l) since I haue passed the
greatest part of my life in such
thinges as these, to the displeasure of our Lord, I do now for
the better pleasing of him, passe
this tyme of my death, in a mis-
liking remembrance of the same.
And if it be troublesome to your
Reuerence, as I know it is, so often to heare my so many offences; do you remember once for
all, that this soule, is, of a sin-

(l) How
desirous
this
soule
was, to
make
God a-
mends.

H 5   ner,

ner, for whome Chriſt dyed.

     Nay ſaid I, if your Lord-
„ ſhip, haue any ſuch appre-
„ henſion, you may repeate
„ as much, and as often as
„ it pleaſeth you ; for I only
„ aduiſed you of it before, as
„ thinking that perhaps you
„ might haue done it by er-
„ rour. *The errour (ſayth he)*
was myne, and a grieuous errour
it was, to offend them ſo many
wayes, who did euer ſtand in
my defence. But howſoeuer that
be ; in this reſpect, as in ſome o-
thers, I ſhall dye contented, in
that I can neuer ſatisfy my ſelfe,
with

with cōfeſſing my faults to you,
deare Father. VVhich now, by
the goodnes of God, are as well
knowne by me, as heeretofore
they were little eſteemed; & are
now as bitterly lamēted, as heer-
tofore they gaue me guſt, though
it were a falſe one. I (m) wish,
Othou moſt ſweet Sauiour of my
ſoule, that I had, as wel, a thouſand tongues, that ſo I might
fully confeſſe them; a thouſand
eyes, that ſo, I might bitterly
bewayle them; and a thouſand
harts, that ſo, eternally I might
deteſt them. And that this grief
for my ſinnes, committed againſt
God.

(m) The man did euen melt be-tweene griefe & loue.

God, might so breake my hart ; as the instrument of Iustice, will take my head, for them, which I haue committed concerning men.

I do, good Father, (by the goodnes of God) know what a sinner I am. As a sinner, I lamēt my selfe, and as a sinner I will dye, but a sinner, all humbled, & contrite ; and with my teares I will make my Funeralls ; then suffer me to performe them, after myne owne fashion. And heer euen I, not (n) being able to containe my selfe from weeping, he obserued it, and said thus. *Most happy Funerals are*

(n) I cannot blame him,

*aretherfore thefe of mine, which
are folemnized by the feruãts of
God. Yet this part belonges not
to you, but only as being a Father to my foule. VVho knowes,
but that by thefe mutuall teares,
and this exchange of tendernes,
my impure confcience may indeed be cleanfed?* Thus both
of vs, being filent for a
while, he then proceeded:
*VVell, my good Father, it is
now high time, that by the* (o)
*Authority, which God hath
giuen you,* to loofe, *and bind
men on earth, you loofe me,
from fo many chaines of finne,*
which

(o) This authori-
ty, was
giuen to
his true
Church
by Iefus
Chrift
our
Lord; &
in his
name, &
by his
power,
it is exer-
cifed;

which hang vpon me. To the end that, as you háue taught me, I may ſay, Auditui meo dabis gaudium & lætitiam, & exultabunt oſſa humiliata. *And firſt do you giue me* Abſolution, *and then, I may performe my* Pennance. *Though indeed what* Pennance, *carrying proportion to my ſinnes, is your* Reuerence *able to impoſe.* At this, he caſt himſelfe at my feete, and bowed his head to my knee, where I had layd my left hand; and he all bathed it with teares, and kiſſed it; and expected the

the *Penance* and *Abſolution*.
Which I gaue him, fully,
in forme of a (p) *Plenary Iu-*
biley, according to the moſt
ample priuiledges, (q) which
are granted to them of that
Congregation, which is called
of the (r) *Miſericordia*. Being
abſolued, and hauing done
his *Pennance*, with incredible affection of mind, he
ſate downe againe by my
direction; and then, the
reſt did come, and circle
him in round about, after
the

(p) This is an application of the ſuperabundant merits of Ieſus Chriſt our Lord, to the ſoules which ſtand in need thereof.

(q) By the Popes.

(r) It is called a
congregation of *Miſericordia*, becauſe it is ſo great a worke of charity & mercy. wherupon they imploy themſelues.

the accuſtomed manner .

I then ſpake firſt to him
" after this ſort:Moſt Illuſtri-
" ous Lord *Troilo* , our *Bleſſed*
" *Sauiour* I E S V S *Chriſt*,whom
" here we haue preſent , did ,
" by dying vpon the *Croſſe* ,
" giue remedy, in his perſon,
" this night,to three thinges,
(s) An   amongſt many others . He
applica-   (s) dyed , in the flower , &
tion full
of life &   vigour of his youth ; that
comfort·   your Lordſhip , might not
" haue too much tendernes ,
" & compaſſion of your owne
" tender youth, and ſo might
" ſay, *O,but why is my life taken*
away

away in so tender years? And „
this is the first . He dyed , ‚,
and he dyed of a violent ‚‚
death ; that to your Lord- ‚‚
shippe it might not seeme „
insupportable , to dye vpon ‚
necessity, and so you might ‚,
say , O, *but why is the flower of* ‚,
my yeares , cut off by a violent „
hand? and this is the second. „
He dyed of the most re- ‚‚
proachfull death , which in ‚‚
those times was inflicted ; ‚‚
that it might not seeme „
strang to your Lordship , „
to dye by the hand of *Iustice,* ‚‚
and so you might say , O , ‚‚

„ but why died not I in my cradle,
„ or at least by some other natural
„ accident?

„   Nay, if your Lordship
„ will accept this death, in so
„ tender yeares, you offer
„ him the best part of your
„ tyme. By dying of a violent
„ death, you may make that
„ which is necessary, to be
„ voluntary; and by dying of
„ a dishonourable death, (ta-
„ king it as a Pennance for
„ your sinnes) you may fly
„ the shame, of that last terri-
„ ble day. And so much the
„ better, you may accept therof,

of, for that you are not to
dye in publique, vpon the
Bridge, as the ordinary
Custome beares ; but (t)
priuately heere below, in
the Court, as is wont to be
vsed, towards your Peeres.
I added also some other có-
siderations, & so ended my
speach. To which the *Barõ*,
who was euer ready, made
this answere.

And (u) *I, O Father, for
as much as concernes the first,
dye willingly in this fresh age of
myne ; because thus I shalbe sure*
not

I 2

make a very yong man, vpon a suddaine.

(t) It is there accounted of lesse dishonour, to be put priuatly to death. They who dye priuatly, dye within the Castle, they who publikely, at the foot of the Bridge.

(u) How wise, the grace of God, is able to

not to offend my Lord , *any*
more. And , from this inſtant, I
offer him my yeares, my age, &
my life ; and a hundred yeares ,
and a hundred ages , and a hun-
dred liues . As for the ſecond ;
I will make a vertue of neceſſity ;
and being to dye perforce , and
according to reaſon ; I will dye
willingly , that ſo I may yield
willingly , vnto force , & wil-
lingly giue ſatisfaction to rea-
ſon. But as for the third ; I could
wiſh for a more ignominious
death . And be you pleaſed to
know , that to haue dyed in pu-
blique, would haue giuen me I
know

know not what increaſe of conſolation, & guſt. For ſo I might
haue hoped by x) *publique Pen-*
nance , to haue made a better a-
mendes, for my publique crimes.
And God doth know, that I take
no contentment , to receaue the
fauour of dying priuately . But
yet howſoeuer , if the determi-
nation which is made, be ſuch ; I
reſiſt it not . Our Lord will accept the promptitude of my wil.

(x) Be-
cauſe
publike
ſinnes ,
require
publike
ſatisfa-
ction.

Heereupon, the *Proue-*
ditore tooke vp the ſpeach ,
and ſayd : Let your Lord-
ship accommodate it ſelfe, „
to the will, and prouidence „

I 3   of

" of God ; who hath not only
" one way , of ariuing to ſaue
" our ſoules , nor one only
" means of drawing them to
" him . He leadeth one by
" one meanes, and others by
" another . It importeth not
that (y) his Iudgmentes be
hidden from vs, but it ſuffi-
ceth that they are iuſt. Who
can tell , if your Lordſhip
ſhould haue dyed in any
other ſort thē this, whether
or no, you ſhould haue bin
ſaued? *I am he (*ſayth the Baron *) who can tell you that ; for
I ſhould haue tumbled headlong
into hell .*   *Do*

(y) Ma-
ny of
Gods
iudge-
ments
areſecret
butthey
are all
iuſt.

Do you not know how God hath proceeded with me? It is iust as a Huntes-man would do, when he would take a wild beast, but he would haue him brought to his hand, whole, and found; and not to be torne by the teeth or pawes of doggs; nor strocken by the bow, nor bruized by nets, or snares. He driues this beast, sometymes one way, and some-tymes another; but neuer lets slip the doggs, nor dischargeth the arrow; nor spreads he the net, or Toyle vpon the ground, or sets the snare; but, at the most, with some outcryes, or els

I 4   *by*

by throwing of some stones, he
rowseth him, and addresseth
him towardes the place designed;
& so long doth he driue the beast
by seuerall wayes, that, at last,
he bringes him thither, where
he would haue him. The Hun-
tes-man knowes this well; and
did long expect him there; & he
takes him, and enioyes him, all
sound, and safe.

(z) Note
how
wittily,
and pi-
ously,
he ma-
kes this
applica-
tion to
himself.

    I am (z) *he, O my Good*
Iesus, who haue beene this beast,
hunted hither, and thither; but
thou hadst a mind, to haue me
safe; thou hadst a mind to haue
me sound. And so thou didst not
per-

permit, that I should be torne with dogs, nor pierced by arrow, nor taken by nets, or Toyles, or snares; when thou deliueredst me out of so many dangers of death, in which, though very young, I haue found my selfe; & wherin, if I had dyed, without faile, I had perished for all eternity. Thou didst only throw stones at me, and thou cryedst out after me, when by so many admonitions, and inspirations, thou didst solicite me. And now I repent my selfe, that I was so deafe to them. But what mer-uaile, if I were deafe, who after

I 5   *a sort*

(a) By
finne

a fort was (a) *dead? And thus
hath his goodnes conducted me to
this ftraite pace , without my
knowing of it ; that fo I may be
forced to leap into his lapp . For
whither am I able to turne my
felfe more fecurely, then to my
deare Iefus? Yea , and yet , if I
were able; I would not turne, a-
ny way but to him . It is true ,
that I am forced; but yet I am
content withall .*

One of the *Confortatori*
,, then replied : It is inough,
,, *Signor Troilo* . So great , and
,, fo liberall, is the goodnes of
,, God, that he accepteth all,
and

and he doth it with delight. ,,
And one of the *Chiesa nuoua* ,,
said ; That although our "
Lord receaued a *Precept* , or "
Commandment that he should ,,
dye ; yet neuerthelesse it is "
affirmed , & it is true, that "
he dyed *voluntarily* . And (b) That
hauing accompanied this punishment
speach of his , with diuers which is
choice examples , one of by ne-
imposed
our Fathers shut vp that cessity,
discourse , with shewing, by made
voluntary,
what means, that which was ry , by a
necessary , (b) might so grow voluntary ac-
to be *voluntary*, by *a volunta-* ceptati-
ry accepting of it: and, that of.
on ther-

so

so much more , it would be *meritorious,* as it should more *willingly* be imbraced . *Then teach me* (fayd the *Baron*) *how I may make this neceſſary death truly voluntary* . And then certaine deuout , and apt waies how to do it, being declared , by the *Gouernour* of the *Congregation* of the *Confortatori* , and imbraced by the *Baron* , I faid ; Perhaps " *Signor Troilo* , we weary you " to much . *How can you weary me ?* faid he. *Theſe diſcourſes, make the night short to me , and they make my diſaſtre,fortunat.*

And

And heere, all were silent for a while; when he rising vp (for he was sitting) said, *That he would speake with the Father*. And drawing neere me, the (c) *Confortatore* said the *Confiteor*; &, that being ended, *I desire (saith he) if it pleaſe you, Father, to call againe to mind, ſome of the things aforſaid; both for the better repetition of them, & for the additiō of ſome others*. Which I refuſing, out of the aſſurance I had, that it was not neceſſary, he said; *And it is poſſible, deare Father, that you will*

(c) Whome the patient, did accompany therin.

will not giue me this last content-
ment? VVill you not permitt,
at least, that I may satisfiy my
selfe, with confessing the offen-
ces, which I haue committed
against God? And besides, doth
not your Reuerence remember,
that we must speake togeather of
(d)pennance? And I answe-
red, Let that *Pennance* be,
to dye, and to dye well.

(d) The
Father,
it seems
had
made
him som
such
promise
before.

   Then teach me that, (said
he.) And I, thus to him:
Offer now, this death of
" yours, to God, with your
" whole hart, in pennance,
" for the sinnes with you
                        haue

haue committed. *I do (saith he) offer it with my hart , and with my mouth ; and it grieues me , (as our Lord doth know) that I haue not , this night, a thousand heades, that in this one of mine, they might be al cut off, and a thousand liues , that they might all be lost . Nay* (e) *I confesse , and know , that euen that pennance , would yet fall short; but since more I cannot , more I know not what to do ; and since more I haue not , I can giue no more ; and euen the doing, and giuing, of this little, do I acknowledge , to proceede from the*

(e) How much doth he giue to God ; & how little doth he thinke it to be; & yet how faythfully doth he acknowledge it all to be of God.

    I told him, by the way
of reply , that it was well;
and that he should still be
doing so . And when (sayd
I) you are laying your head
" vpon the blocke , say thus
" in your hart . O Lord, by
" this act of myne, I protest ,
" to do pennance for my sins,
" as if I had a thousand heads
" and a thousand liues ; and I
" acknowledge, and confesse,
" that it is all but little . But
" I doubt *Signor Troilo* , whe-
" ther then , you willbe able
" to remember this ; for then
                per-

perhapps you willbe , as it "
were, not your self . It is no "
trifle to looke death in the "
face, take my word for that . ,,
The magnanimous Lord "
made this answere . *I wil not* "
presume so much vpon my selfe,
but I (f) *hope well , and confide*
greatly in God, that he will not
let it fall out of my memory .
And if, by many accident, you
should perceaue that I were vn-
worthy of so great a grace , doe
me the fauour to bring me in
mind of it ; for you shall find me
ready to put it in execution . In
the meane whyle, I beseech your

(f) He
can ne-
uer faile
who
putteth
all con-
fidence
in God ,
& none
in him-
selfe .

K   Reue-

*Reuerence tell me somewhat els
towardes this end of myne, and
that quickly, for the tyme hath
winges.* I bad him leaue the
" care of that to me. For I wil
" (sayd I)go intimating from
" time to tyme, whatsoeuer
" you are to thinke vpon; &
" whatsoeuer you shall be to
" say, euē til your last breath.
　　And (g) very now, you

(g) He
exhor-
teth him
toa great
deuotiō
to his
good
Angell.

shall begin to make a
strait friendship with your
Good Angell. And first aske
pardon of him with your
hart, for the little gratitude
" which you haue expressed,
　　　　　　　　　　　for

for the Cuſtody that he ,,
hath affoarded you; which ,,
hath bin ſo inceſſant, ſo pati- ''
ent, ſo diligent, & ſo full of ''
loue: Vpon which wordes , ,,
he ſayd (caſting himſelfe »
vpon his knees;) *Yea , not
only with my mouth, but with
my hart, I begge pardon of him,
for the much, and much ingratitude; which I haue vſed , notwithſtanding his ſo great beni-
gnity , and loue to me; and ſo*
kiſſing my knee , he ſate
downe againe. So that I
proceeded, and ſaid: Conſider then with your ſelfe , "
K 2   that

(h) Saint Hierome sayth expresly, That euery soule hath an *Angelus Custos* assigned to it by Almighty God, from the first instance of the birth till the last of life. *Vide Hier. lib. 3. conc. in 28. cap. Matt.*

that your (h)*good Angel* now is heer, who euen from your very first beginning, when you were borne, & so much more at this houre, which is so full of danger, doth assist you, and especially, in six particulers. First, he hinders the impetuous assaults of the diuell, and weakens the force of all those maligne spirits, who do, at this instant, conspire to the damnation of your soule. Secondly, he brea-

thes

The holy Scriptures and holy Fathers doe also a-bound in proofe of the ministery of Angells in the help of men.

thes into your hart, Pre- „
paration, Generofity, De- „
uotion, and Contrition. „
Thirdly, he lightneth this „
Darcknes, this Anguish, & „
this Death. Fourthly, with „
great follicitude, he carrieth „
foreward, and backward, „
thofe meffages, which paffe „
betweene God and you; he „
gathers vp your fighs, your „
very countenances, and the „
humiliations of your hart; „
there is not one of them , „
which he fuffereth to loofe „
his way. Fiftly, he negotia- „
teth with other Angells of „

(i) We read in holy ſcripture (*Daniel* 10.) how one Angell helpeth another, for the good of men; & both the holy Scriptures, and holy Fathers do euery where abound, with ſhewing the tender care

ſuperiour (i) Quiers, ſo to procure effectual aſſiſtances for your ſaluation. In moſt particuler manner, he moueth S. *Michael* the *Archangell*, that he will defend you in this night. Sixtly, he ſolliciteth my good Angell alſo, that he may procure me to be a competent inſtrument, in this paſſage, which you are making towardes your ſaluation.

Salute him therfore, and ſay thus with me; *Angele Dei,*

O

that the holy Angells haue of all thinges, that concerne vs, either in ſoule, body, or goods.

O (k) thou Angell of God, so ill knowne, and so ill vsed by me, *qui custos es mei*, who keepest me, with so continual care, and perfect loue, *me tibi commissum*, who am committed to thee, being a man so faulty, and brought by the prouidence of God to this passage; but yet a sinner who by his mercy, & thy prayers is contrite for his sinnes, *pietate superna*, by the goodnes of God, for

(k) He pondereth the prayer which Catholikes say dayly, & more often then so, to their good Angell: *Angele Dei, qui custos es mei, me tibi commissum, pietate superna, hodie illumina,*

K 4   I

custodi, rege, guberna. O thou Angell of God, who art my keeper, appointed by the goodnes of God, illuminate me, this day, preserue me, rule and gouerne me. Amen.

« I find no defert, but do cor-
« dially confesse much deme-
« rit *in hac morte, & hac nocte*,
« in this death, which is due
« to me for my offences, & in
« this laft period of my life,
« *illumina, custodi, rege, & gu-*
« *berna*, do thou illuminate,
« defend, protect, and gouerne me, *Amen*. This good
Noble Man, did repeate
thefe wordes, with affectuous and abundant teares; &
euen by his countenance,
one might fee, his very hart
fplit in his body. And not
contenting himfelfe, to fay
                              it

it only once , he would needs repeate it then, three times; and afterwarde s, he did it againe, so much more often , the same night , as that all the times ariued, I thinke, to ten ; letting me know withall, that he had not felt greater solace , and gust, in any one spirituall exercise, then in this .

Secondly (sayd I) you shal take the Glorious Virgin , for your (l) intercessour; and then *S. Iohn* the *Baptist*, and *S. Paul*, who were both, condéned to the

(l) To pray for him , as one man may do for another; though all the Saints, & much more, the glorious Mother of God, do performe it, in a far more excellent manner.

K 5   losse

" loſſe of their heads, as your
" Lordſhip is . *It is true (ſayd*
he) that they were condemned
as I am;but with this difference,
That they ſuffered innocent, &
I for my faults ; and therefore I
I accuſe my ſelfe , of ſuch , and
ſuch, and ſuch offences , which I
haue committed againſt God .
VVhich howſoeuer I confeſſed
before, yet for the reaſons which
I haue already touched, I do wil-
lingly repeate the ſame . After
he had ended his *Confeſſion ,*
and receaued *Abſolution* vpon his knees , I deſired him
to ſit down againe, that the
wonted

wonted company might
come about him.

And euer, some one of
them, would be taking vp,
some verse of the *holy Scrip-*
ture, which might be ap-
propriated to the present
occasion. As for example,
Viam iniquitatis amoue à me, &
de lege tua miserere mei. Suscipe
seruum tuum in bonum, & iusti-
ficationes tuas edoce me. Bonum
mihi, quia humiliasti me, vt dis-
cam iustificationes tuas. Cogno-
ui Domine, quia æquitas iudicia
tua, & in veritate tua humilia-
sti me. Fiat cor meum.immacu-
latum

*latum in iustificationibus tuis, vt non confundar . Miserere mei Deus, secundum magnam misericordiam tuam , & secundum multitudinem miserationum tuarum , dele iniquitatem meam. Errauifîcut ouis quæ perijt, quære seruum tuum Domine . Deus propitius esto mihi peccatori . Deus in adiutorium meum in-*tende. And a hundred other, such as these; which now, and then, were declared by some one of (m) vs, according to the present occasiõ, wherin he tooke much contentment .

(m) The *Religious* men declared them, though the *Confortatori* might represét them .

But

But (n) especially he had great cōfort, in vsing these other Iaculatory Prayers, *Maria mater gratiæ, Mater misericordiæ, Tu nos ab hoste protege, & hora mortis suscipe;* repeating often these last wordes, *& hora mortis suscipe.* And againe; *Eia ergo aduocata nostra, illos tuos misericordes oculos ad nos conuerte, & Iesum benedictum fructum ventris tui, mihi, post hanc noctem, ostende, O clemens, O pia, O dulcis Virgo Maria. Ora pro me peccatore indigno, in hac hora mortis meæ, Amen, Amen, Amē.*

(n) He was most tenderly deuoted to the B. Virgin.

Recor-

Recordare Iesu pie , Quod sim causa tuæ viæ, Ne me perdas illa die &c. In this exercise, those brothers, of the *Congregation* of the *Misericordia*, were very perfect , and discreete ; deliuering out, in fit times, a greate number of these versicles , without importuning , or perplexing him. And so also did other Religious men, according to the occasion , without either interrupting the one the other , or yet ouerweariyng the yong Noble Man ; and they also brought thinges

so,

so, as to accompany them
with certaine motiues, and
considerations, with bre-
uity, but with great life of
deuotion.

When these thinges
were ended, I said: It will „
not be amisse that we recite „
the *Letanies*, if these Gentle-„
men shall thincke it fit. „
And I (said the yong Lord)
if you, and they be so contented,
will be he, that shall recite them.
They all made answere in
the negatiue, saying to him;
Your Lordshippe, would „
but weary your selfe, too „
much

much . *Nothing leſſe* , (ſaid
he) *but to me it will be, of ex-*
treame contentment . And ſo ,
(w^{th}out more diſpute) they
put the book into his hand;
and (kneeling euen , by
me , againſt a fourme) he
began the *Letanyes*,to which
we anſwearing , *Ora pro eo* ,
Pray for him , there (o) was
not a man amongſt vs, who
accompanied not the words
of his mouth with the tears
of his eyes. And eſpecially,
when with incredible af-
fection, and deuotion , he
repeated , theſe wordes , *A*
                    mala

(o) It
muſt
needes,
be an
obiect of
great
compaſ-
ſion.

mala morte, A potestate diaboli,
A pœnis inferni , libera me Do-
mine. Deliuer me , O Lord from
an euill death , from the power
of the diuell , and from the tor-
mentes of hell . But (p) he (O
admirable repose of that
mind) did not shead one
teare. Nay my selfe being in
teares, who held vp the can-
dle by him (and not being
able to represse them) he
stirred me with his elbow ,
and made other signes to
them, that so , giuing o-
uer their weepinge , they
might answere him . And

L   spea-

(p) No-
thing
but only
his sins
could
moue
him to
teares.

speaking of it to me afterward, he said, *That there wanted little, of their making him also weep, for company.*

When the *Letanies* were ended, he sayd (turning to me) *Father, say you the prayers ouer me, that follow.* And then, he tooke the light out of my hand, and so giuing me the booke, I said those praiers ouer him, which are wont to be said, ouer such as are in their last agony; *Commēao* (q) *te omnipotenti dèo &c.* And that other which followeth, *Deus misericors, Deus*

(q) Thefe are as admirable and affectuous praiers, as any are vfed in the whol office of the holy Church; and I wish all the Readers of this, to procure to fee & reade them.

Deus clemens &c. And at the end of these, he sayd with a loud voice, the *Pater Noster,* the *Aue maria,* the *Credo,* & the *Salue Regina* ; and so he returned to sit downe , the others making the accusto- med circle about him. And so one , with representing some sentence of *Holy Scrip- ture,* another, some exam- ple , another , some other spirituall Consideration , we alwaies kept him aliue, and quicke , and euen all kindled in deuotion ; till such time, as the houre of

L 2   cele-

celebrating *Masse*, approached.

Then the Noble Man sayd thus: *If these (r) maniacles be put vpon me to giue me payne, or punishment, let the will of my Prince be done, who is pleased to haue it so; but if the meaning be, but to make me sure; in vaine is he tyed without, who is bound (s) within.* Vpon which wordes, all of vs being full (t) of tendernes; and in particuler one of those *Confortatori* (who shew-

(r) This rigour is vsed in those partes, for the great insolencies which haue sometyms been expressed, in the like extremityes, by delinquents.

(s) Because his hart was more chained, by the loue of God, then his handes could be, by a load of yron.

(t) They had great reason.

shewed himselfe, through-
out that whole night , as a
moſt compaſſionate Gen-
tleman , in ſeruice of this
Noble Man) cauſed the
keyes to be inſtantly giuen
him , and ſo tooke the manicles off; which yet , the
Baron would needs (u) kiſſe,
and kiſſing them, he ſighed,
and ſo held his peace .

(u) An
humble,
naturall,
& moſt
Noble
Soule.

When he had been ſilent
a while , and hauing made
a ſigne that he deſired to
confeſſe againe ; and when
he had bleſſed himſelfe,
with the ſigne of the *Croſſe* ;

L 3   *Father*

(x) He is
much
folicited
by the
memory
of his
difobe-
dience
to his
Mother.

Father (x), (fayd he) *I who*
haue giuen fo many difguftes,
and fo bitter ones, to my moft
deare Lady, & Mother, through
the whole courfe of my life; what
comfort doth your Reuerence
thinke, that I might be able to
giue her in my death? By dy-
„ ing wel (fayd I) & in a holy
„ manner. To which he an-
fwered thus; *How shall the vn-*
fortunate woman come to know
it? I told him, that I would
„ relate it to her by word of
„ mouth; and in fine I would
„ write it for her; and I will
„ not only notify it (fayd I)

to

to her, but to any other whome it may import to know it. *It is inough,* (fayd he) & he reached his hands out to me, that I might giue him one of myne, and with-all, my word. And fo he kiffed it often, and holding it betweene both his, he continued to fpeake after this manner

I could wish, deare Father, that in my place, your Reuerence would often vifit and comfort my Lady my Mother, after my death. And when fo, you fhal fee her firft, I defire that you

L 4 *will*

*will aske for giuenes of her in my
name, a thousand, and a thousand tymes, as heer I haue done,
both now, and the other day,
since I came to prison. And especially, begge pardon of her,
for such, and such a particuler
offence, and then say to her thus;*
Your *Troilus* who is dead,
begs that blessing frō your
most afflicted Ladishippe,
which being aliue, he neither deserued, nor had time
to aske. He further recom-
mendes the care of his soule
to your Ladiship. He prai-
eth, he beseecheth, he con-
iureth.

iureth your Ladiship , to
graunt him this his laſt &
now only ſuite; that hauing
put your ſoule in peace, you
will not ſo much as reſent ,
or call to mind , and much
leſſe procure to (y) reuenge
your ſelfe , for any iniury ;
but that you will remit the
whole, and your ſelfe withall , to the Eternall Prouidence of God . *Put her in*
mind , that it is the part of a
Roman, *and* Chriſtian *hart,*
after a generous manner to par-
don offences . And , giuing her
all comfort , do you aſſure her ,

(y) If ſhe
thought
that the
aduerſe
parties ,
whome
he had
wron-
ged , had
proſecu-
ted him
with too
much
eager-
nes .

L 5   *that*

that I haue particulerly reuer-
sed, all those irreuerent words,
that I haue formerly vsed towardes her ; and that I haue
remembred all those most sweet,
deare benefits , which I haue
receaued from her ; and all those
Maternall fauours , which she
hath vouchsafed me . And a-
boue all, let her know , the ine-
stimable contentment that I haue
to thincke of the (z) *Christian*
loue, which she hath expressed to
me, in this last passage ; without
euer reflecting vpon those offences, and great demerits of myne.
      Say to her moreouer, that
                          I dye

(z) This
was a
Mother,
not only
of her
sonnes
body,
but of
his soule
also.

I dye her sonne, & a sonne, who
is most profoundly penitent, for
all the ill wordes, and deeds that
I haue euer vttered, and performed against her; and that, in
the other world; I will by Gods
grace, be as gratefull to her, as
I haue beene vngratefull, heer.
Relate to her my last passage, in
most particuler manner; and o-
blige her, liberally to reward al
my followers, who haue been in
prison, vpon my occasion. Of
whome, I doe with all the very
bowells of my hart, aske pardon,
for the payne, and perill, wher-
into I did idly, and absurdly cast
them.

them. And assure her, in a word, that if for nothing els, yet euen for the very disgustes which I haue giuen to her, I shall dye content; finding a kind of ioy in my hart, that I performe this pennance, in this manner, which I haue so well deserued. And so, I dying in such sort, as your Reuerence may be pleased to let her know, she cannot but receaue some côfort in my death; and she will also find, that she is euen engaged, so to range her selfe to the will of God, as, by his mercy, I haue done.

To my Lady, my Grand-
Mother

Mother, what shall I say, deere Father? O how compassiue am I of her great age! VVhat paine doth my soule feele, for that paine of hers! Giue her also to vnderstand, that I begge pardon of her, for so many disgustes, as, in this old age of hers, I haue giuen her; beseeching her in my name, that as long as she shall liue, she will weekly, cause a Masse to be celebrated, for my soule. And in like māner I humbly aske pardon of my Lord Marquesse, my Vncle, from the most inward parts of my soule, as I also doe of the rest of my bloud

bloud; befeeching them all to excufe this youth, or rather ignorance of myne. Putting alfo thē
in mind, that once we shal al meet
in heauen. And if euer your Reuerence can procure to be in my
Caftles, aske pardon, I befeech
you, in my name, a hundred
tymes, of all my vaffalls. Making a promife to them, that in-
fteed of the ill example which I
haue giuen them, I will not forget them in heauen, when by the
mercy of God, I shall be there;
and let them, in the meane tyme,
excufe my youth.

Forget not alfo to do this
office,

office , with (a) Monsig.ʳ the Gouernour of Rome , who about some foure tymes, hath examined me, with so much respect and courtesy . Giuing him assurance , from me, that although my death do grieue me, yet I accept willingly thereof . And beseeching him , that, when tyme shall serue, he wil also (b) assure our Lord, Pope Clement, his Holynes, that I dye his most deuoted Sonne ; and most satisfyed, with the proceeding of his Holynes, towardes me . VVith this moreouer , that I am grieued at the very rootes of

my

(a) This was a person of great authority and place, who took his examination.

(b) vvith how great piety, he speakes of the Pope, as he was his supreme Pastour, & with obseruance as of his Prince.

(c) A
noble
circum-
stance of
ciuiltty,
and cur-
tesy.

my (c) *hart, for hauing giuen his*
Holynes, *so much cause of
trouble, and griefe; especially in
this beginning of his* Pontifi-
cate, *and in the middeſt of the
ioy, which hath beene expreſſed
for his aſſumption, to the* Sea
Apoſtolique. *And let him be
further told, that by placing my
selfe, as I doe at your feet, I
make accoumpt, that I lay my
head ⸿vnder the feet of his* Holynes; *that so he may vouch-
safe to giue me his benediction.
I hauing this comfort, in the
midſt of all my afflictions, that
his ſentence, and my death, will
            ſerue*

serue to his whole State, for a lawfull, and plentifull example of his Iustice. And verily, if it grieue me, at this tyme, to dye, it doth also grieue me, that euen by my death, I am not able to giue complete satisfaction, to his Holynes. *For* (d) *as much as he, being my Father, and my Pastour, he cannot, in fine, but feele the death of a Sonne, and sheep, of his, with displeasure, and griefe.*

(d) what a noble ciuill Soule was this?

Vpon which wordes, he finding, (euen more then before) that there fell some teares from mine eyes, to

M   his

his handes, *This is well in-*
deed, (ſayd he) *your* Reuerence, *commendes my courage ;*
but why then do you weepe your
ſelfe? At leaſt, let not others
ſee you . Then I replying
" ſaid . Do you belieue , my
" Sonne, that I haue no fee-
" ling in me ? Do you thinke
" perhaps, that I am ſome
" piece of marble ? Proceed
" you on to the reſt . And
then, naming diuers of his
particuler friendes , he deſired me to aske pardon for
him , of them all ; and this
he did , with wordes of
ex-

extreame ſweetenes , and
prudence. This being then
ſaid by him with a moſt ad-
mirably intrepide hart , he
concluded with this deſire ;
I beſeech your Reuerence ,
*that in the laſt place , you will
begge pardon for me, of Almighty God , as I my ſelfe do now,
with the moſt internall part of
my hart; and of your ſelfe , I
aske my* Pennance , *and* Abſolution .

Which as ſoone as I had
giuen him , the Brothers of
that *Congregation* of the *Miſericordia,* did put vs in mind
how

how it was tyme that *Maſſe*
should be celebrated; and
ſo the Prieſt, as ſoone as he
was veſted, began. The deuout yong Lord, & I knee-
ling togeather againſt a
fourme, he ſayd thus to me.
The Prieſt is beginning Maſſe;
*& I (with your good leaue) wil
haue a new* Reconcilation,
*according to that, which my
Good Angell shall bring to my
remembrance, of whome I haue
deſired this fauour.* The *Prieſt*
was ſaying the *Confiteor* at
the foote of the *Altar*; to
whome one of the *Congregation*

tion (making anſwere) was
ſo ouerwrought with ten-
dernes, that he could not
get to the end of it; in ſuch
ſort, as that it was neceſſary, that ſome other ſhould
doe it for him. Then the
good Noble Man, who an-
ſwered ſoftly to the *Cōſiteor*,
leaning towardes me, ſayd
thus, *Giue*(e) *me leaue to weep,*
whyleſt I ſay the Confiteor,
ſince that Gentleman weepes ſo
bitterly, to whoſe office it belon-
geth not greatly, that he ſhould
weep. I anſwered, that he „
might weep in the name of »

(e) He
had the
guift of
teares, in
a ſtrange
meaſure.

M 3   God;

" God ; since he had giuen
" him ſo great deſire ſo to do.
And it was an admirable effect of diuine grace, that inſtantly, I ſaw the tears ſtrea-
ming downe his cheekes,
and powring themſelues, e-
uen vpon the cushion, that
lay beſore him .

When the *Confiteor* was
done , and all (f) the whyle
that the *Prieſt* was reading
with a loud voice , he did
not mooue at all, but was
moſt fixedly attentiue , and
as it were rapt towards the
(g)*Crucifixe*, vpon the *Altar*,
which

(f) Till
after the
Ghoſ-
pell .
(g) The
Crucifixe
was of
ſtone, or
wood,
but his
mind
was v-
pon the
Original
and not
vpon the
picture,
which
was but
a picture
or Ima-
ge.

which was there moſt deuo-
utly made . And ſhortly after , turning towards myne
eare, he accuſed himſelfe of
diuers little thinges, which
ſuddenly then did ſurprize
his mind . And the *Prieſt*
being come to (h) *Surſum cor-* (h) A-
da ; *Father* (ſayd he) *do you* bout the
thinke indeed , that by ſuch a middle
death as this, and ſo well deſer- of Maſſe.
ued, I may yet go ſtraight to
heauen ? And why not (ſayd »
I) with ſo great and ſo well »
conditioned affectuouſnes »
of mind, might your Lord- »
ſhip vndergo this death, as »
     M 4   that

« that your soule would be
« sure to flye vp inftantly,
« from the blocke, into heauen. *O my God!* (fayd he) *And
what kind of affectuoufnes muft
that be! O teach it me a little!
O that our Lord, would graunt
it to me!* Pray (fayd I) very
« earneftly vnto him for it,
« and peraduenture he will
« graunt it. At which tyme,
the *Prieft* being in the very
act of the *Eleuation of the body of our Lord,* the yong Noble Man, fpake thefe very,
very wordes *. O bone Iefu, fis
mihi, in hac hora, Iefus. O deare
Lord*

Lord Iefus , be thou , in this houre, a Iefus to me. And this he fayd, with fo ardent affection of mind, though with a low voice, as that after it, he was wholy immoueable, till the *Priest* went on, to (i) *Domine non fum dignus, &c* . And then , he fayd thus to me . *I haue not , Father , beene attentiue,either when the* Pater Nofter *, or the* Agnus Dei *, was fayd ;may I yet neuerthelesse communicate?* I anfwered, that for the prefent , he should do fuch a (k) pennance, whilest I was giuing

(i) The later end of Maffe.

(k) This was perhaps, the knocking of his breaft, or fome fuch other thing, which might be done at the inftant.

M 5   him

him *Abſolution* . Which being done , he went , of himſelfe , to the *Altar* ; and
kneeling downe , did with
exemplar deuotion, receaue
the *moſt Bleſſed Sacrament* ; &
ſoone after , he came backe
from *Maſſe* , towardes me ,
where he remained , with-
out any motion at all .

After this , turning
about to all them who did
aſſiſt , he ſaid , *I giue thankes*
to you all , for your Charity and
courteſy ; and pardon , I beſeech
you , the painfull night , which I
haue brought vpon you . And
                                then

then, he defired me, for
the loue of him, to repeate
thofe wordes, to euery one
of them, in particuler; and
fo I did. Being thē intreated
to fit downe, the wonted
circle was made about him.
Where euery one procured,
to animate him, towardes
that combat which was thē
at hand; by reprefenting
the shortnes of the paine,
the imméfity of the reward,
the vanity of the world;
& aboue all, the aboundant
grace, which, in the fpace
of fo few houres, our Lord
                    had

had communicated to his foule; and had giuen him with all, fuch a pregnant figne of his *Predeftination*; wherein the Noble Youth, did (1) fhew to find extraordinary guft.

Amongft the many difcourfes which were made to this purpofe, as wel by the *Confortatori*, as by our Fathers, I vfed this. And " what thinke you, *Signor* " *Troilo*, will the grace which " God hath giuen you, be " fufficient to make you beare " this punifhment? Nay I tell you

(1) And fo he might moft iuftly doe.

you , that in imitation of "
Chriſt , you should do well "
to deſire it , and that deſire, "
would ſerue to make it , a "
ſmall matter , to you . Nay "
it would make it ſeeme no "
punishment at all ; & laſtly "
it would make it ſeeme "
ſweet . Euen as it hapned to
Chriſt our Lord himſelfe ,
to (m) whom his *Paſſion* ,
ſeemed ſo ſmall a matter ,
that whereas others called
it , by the name of a huge
thing, an *Ocean,* a deep ſea,
(*Veni in altitudinem maris, &*
tempeſtas demerſit me) himſelf

(m) The immenſe loue which our lord Ieſus bare to man, made all that he ſuffered, ſeeme little to him.

doth

" doth call it, but a Cupfull;
" (*Calicem quem dedit mihi pater,*
" *non vis vt bibă illum?*) Againe,
" after that huge heape of
" bitternes, and tormentes
" which he had endured, it
" feemed nothing to him. For
" being asked by thofe dif-
" ciples who were going to
" *Emaus*, if he knew of that
" vaft cruelty, which had
" lately then, bin executed at
" *Hierufalem*, vpon the perfon
" of the greateft Saint ofGod;
" he anfweared, by asking,
" *Quæ?* for in fine he efteemed
" it all as nothing . Therefore

fore speaking of his *Passion*,,
he vsed the word *Baptisme*,,
saying, *Baptismo habeo bap-*
tizari, et quomodo coarctor &c.
And you know that *bathes*
do serue for delicacy. What
say you then *Signor Troilo* ?
Doth not your punishe-
ment by this time, seeme
small to you ? *Small; (saith*
he?) it seemeth nothing. Yet can
I not say, either that it is no-
thing, or yet very pleasant;
but yet neuerthelesse, it is deare
to me, and as such I prize it.
And (n) *I do assure you, that at*
the present, it would be as it
were

(n) How
mightily
this no-
ble man,
grew vp
in grace,
euen by
momēts,

(o) This
so ardent
desire, of
suffering
for his
sinnes,
must
needs be
a great
disposici-
tion to-
wardes
the ob-
tayning:
of par-
don for
them,
through
the mer-
cy of
Christ
our
Lord.

were, *a kind of trouble for me,*
to escape it. Before I desired to
escape; I sighed for it; I laboured
for it; and I know not what of
that kind. But I had not then,
that knowledg of my selfe, which
now, by the fauour of God, me
thinkes I haue; in such sort,
that now, I can affirme to you,
in the worde of Truth, that I
(o) desire my end, how painfull
soeuer it may be, towardes the
remission of my sinnes.

'To this, another Father
..said; "Your Lordship spea-
"keth wisely; for in fine, God
"knoweth, whether other-
wise,

wife, you should euer haue „
beene fo well prepared for »
death. Whereupon, one of »
the *Confortatori* proceeded,
faying: If your Lordship „
had dyed naturally in your „
bed;what, with the paine of „
your body, and the anguish »
of your mind;it may be you „
would fcarce haue beene „
maifter of your felfe. And „
if you had dyed, by any o- „
ther accident, perhaps you (p) Sup-
would not haue had time, poſing
to bring forth, fo much as grace of
the name of *Iefus*. Whereas God, as
now, it (p) is in a manner, red af-
            N   in terward.

" in your owne power, to dye
" as well as you will , your
" selfe ; with what greife of
" your sinnes you will ; with
" what loue of chrift you will;
" and, in a word , in that beft
" manner, which the grace of
" Almighty God will impart
" to you ; which we perceaue,
" euen fo to ouerflow your
" foule , that we are as much
" aftonished , as comforted ,
" by the knowledge therof.

Heereunto the conftant
Noble Man , made this an-
fwere . *You shall know, that by*
the goodnes of God, I find not in
my

my selfe, any trouble, or tentation; and me (q) thinkes I am in a hand which beares me vp. I desire, and I resolue to dye, in that manner, which I shall be taught to be the best; and I am most ready, to obey in all that, which for the sauing of my soule shall be commanded me. This, said I, you shal therfore do. You shal barre you selfe, in that houre, of some ease. 'That is, you shal for the loue of *Iesus,* and, in imitation of what he did and suffered for you, depriue your selfe of somewhat

(q) Nothing but the very hand of God, was able so to haue códucted him, through these stony wayes. And it seemes, that God communicated himselfe to the delinquent, in a very particuler manner.

N 2   **which**

" which you might haue ; and
" which, at that time, might
" be agreeable to you. For, if
" you doe well remember it,
" they gaue twice, vnto our
" Lord, to drinke. The firſt
" time, when they gaue him
" *rinagre*, he drunke; but whé
" they gaue him wine, as ſoon
" as he had taſted it, he put it
" by. But do you know the
" reaſon? It was this. To ſuch
" as were condemned to dye,
" it was the cuſtome to giue
" wine, with an infuſion of
" *myrrhe*; that by the comfort
" thereof, they might faint

the

the leſſe , vnder their tor- „
ments. Now our Lord(who „
was pleaſed to depriue him- „
ſelfe entierly , and fully, of „
all conſolation, for loue of „
vs , and for our example) „
refuſed that , but he accep- „
ted of the *vinagre* , which „
was mingled with (r) ano- ^(r)With Gall .
ther moſt bitter ingredient;
that ſo , he might ſuffer the „
moſt he could; both for our „
example,and benefit other- „
wiſe .

　　The *Proueditore* ſayd ,
that this was moſt certainly „
true; whereupon ſome ex- „

　　　　N 3　　　　pound

„ pound thofe wordes, which
„ Chrift fpake vpon the *croffe*,
„ *Deus Deus meus, vt quid dere-*
„ *liquifti me?* That Chrift our
„ Lord, did greiue thereat,
„ becaufe the *Diuinity*, began
„ as it were, to hide it felfe
„ from the *Humanity* ; & con-
„ fequently by little & little,
„ his life was leauing him ; &
„ by occafion thereof, he
„ was able to fuffer no longer;
„ which the moft enamoured
„ Iefus obferuing, did com-
„ plaine of the matter, to his
„ *Father*, by the wordes afore-
„ fayd.

To

To these thinges a Father of ours, adding other deuout, and short discourses, the *Confortatore* sayd; That for the tyme his soule was sufficiently fed; & that it would be well done, to refresh his body. The Baron answered, *that there was no neede*. But they pressing it much, there was brought in some wine, by a seruant of the Lord (s) *Gouernour* of the *Castle*, which, one of the Gentlemen there present, powring forth into a glasse, presented to the *Baron*; who

N 4   sayd

(s) This Gouernement, is the place of greatest confidéce which the Pope bestowes

sayd again, that it was wholy needles. *And yet* (sayd he,
turning then towardes me)
if I should need it, your (t) *Re-*
uerence told me a whyle agoe,
that in imitation of Chrift, I
should doe well to depriue my
selfe thereof. Father, is it not.
so? Neuertheles, being intreated by al the Affiftants,
that he would drinke, or
at leaft, that he would, so
much, as wash his mouth;
this laft he did twice, without fwallowing any wine at
all . And this was so much
more remarkeable, becaufe
                              fuch

(t) A
good
memory
he had,
and a
more pi-
ous will.

such as are in that cafe, vfe to be extremely taken with thirft, and it is wont to be held, for one of their grea teft torments.

The wine being then carryed away, diuers queftions were asked of this moft Illuftrious Lord, to which he (u) anfwered, with fo great prudence & iudgement, that more could not be imagined. He was asked firft (for, of many, I will mention only a few) & this firft queftion he was asked often;) *Signor Troilo,*

(u) Note & wonder at thefe anfweares, which are fo ful of picty, wifedom and courage.

N 5   will

will your Lordship haue a-
ny thing? He still answered,
that he desired nothing , sauing
that once, he held his peace,
but made a signe vp to heauen. Besides, he was often
asked, *Signor Troilo*, of what
are you thinking? Someti-
mes he aswered, *vpon nothing
in particuler*; Sometimes, *v-
pon our Lord* ; Sometimes ,
vpon my sinnes; Sometimes ,
vpon my approaching end; Som-
times , he sayd, *I thinke vpon
the so many guiftes, which God
hath bestowed vpon me, & that
I haue been, so very vngrateful,*
yea

yea & euen vnmindfull *of them*
all. Being then asked in this
manner, Doth your Lord ,,
ship dye willingly? He an- ,,
swered thus : *And what ?*
would you haue me buftle againft
the order of the Prince? Or
should I not be content, with the
prouidence, and good pleafure of
God? Is it poffible, fayd one, ,,
that the Diuell should not ,,
ftriue, to make you thinke ,,
your death vniuft? *I do not,* ,,
fayth he, *efteeme it only to be*
iuft; but moft iuft; and as for the
Diuell, I neither haue, nor wil
I haue, any more to do with him,

I haue

I haue had inough, and too much of him already .

Another asked him what
" he fayd, of the Lady his
" Mother, his Friendes, his
" Kinred, and himfelfe; if he
" were not much afflicted,
" with the thought thereof?

Concerning my Lady, my Mo-
ther (fayth he) I confeffe, that
in the moft inward partes of my
hart, I find extreme affliction;
but, on the other fide, I reioyce
that I am paying the offences,
that I haue comitted againft her,
with my bloud. And I hope, that
the readines wherewith I im-
brace

brace this pennance, for my wicked carriage towards her, willbe
so well accepted by *Almighty
God*; that he may, through
his goodnes, giue her no small
comfort, euen by this very death
of myne. I thinke vpon my kinred with grief, as hauing been a
cause of payne, and trouble to
them. Of my friends, as hauing
giuen them ill example. Of my
selfe, I take no care; for behold
who (x) doth it for me; making
a signe towards the *Crucifixe,*
which he had hard by him.

(x) A
great
fayth, &
hope, &
loue.

Being asked, whether
the tyme did seeme long to
him

(y) This doe I find to be a strange answere, in the superlatiue degree of strangenes.

him or short? *Neither* (y) *long* (sayth he) *nor short*. And another replying to him thus; Is it possible, that you are not grieued, that you must dye? *I do not* (sayth he) *deny, but that I am grieued at it; but yet it neither troubles me, nor so much as alters me, more thē you see.* It being wished, that he should suffer his chaire, to be drawn a litle forward, that so he might sit at greater ease; *To what end* (sayth he) *should I giue my body ease? I am well heere ; and with the help of God, I shallbe shortly free*

*free , from needing that, or any
thing els* . Being defired to
raife, and reft his feet, vpon
a place of aduantage, where
they vfed to kneele, for that
fo, he should be in a more
commodious pofture ; he
fayd (drawing neer towards
myne eare,)*Father , it is a piece
of ill manners, to fit with a mans
legs raifed vp, in the prefence of
other men* . But I telling him
no, and aduifing him how-
foeuer , that he would fet
them vp; he did inftantly
accommodate himfelfe to
my defire . Being asked , to
what

« what deuotions , he had bin
« moſt particulerly affected:
He anſweared , *To that of*
our (z) *Bleſſed Lady , in whoſe*
honour , I did dayly recite her
Office , but with an impure
mouth; and how then , could that
be accepted by her ? And till
within theſe two yeares, I made
said he , much account of going
to Confeſſion , which through
the mercy of my Lord , I reſol-
ued neuer to intermitt , vnleſſe
it were by ſome very vnlucky
accident, that should haue inter-
poſed it ſelfe . And I euer carri-
ed liuing , in my hart , the me-
mory

(z) He
was euer
much
deuoted
to our
B. Lady.

mory of *manie thinges* , *which formerly* , *vpon feuerall occaf-ons had beene reprefented to me by fundry Religious Fathers* , *with whome I had much conuerfed*, (infinuating therby, as I conceaue, the Fathers of the *Chiefa Nuoua*.) *And when I had meanes, to do it in priuate, I neuer failed any day, to falute the Bleffed Virgin vpon my bare knees*. And then, I faying (I know not well, vpon what occafion) *Ah poore Signor Troilo* . Poore (fayd he) I was, *when I was without the grace of my Lord God, but now, I take*

O   my

my selfe to be rich .

But then the tyme of his end drawing on apace, we rising vp from our seats, did circle him in, vpon our knees. And (after the manner of two Quires, interchangeably answering one another) we began the seauen *Penitentiall Psalms*; pondering some of the verses now and then, and causing him, to resume diuers of them. They being ended, he was aduised to say often, *Eia* (a) *ergo aduocata nostra &c.* And then, *Maria mater gratiæ.*

(a) These are parts of some *Hymnes*, which are recited by the holy Church, in honour of our lord Iesus, & our B. Lady.

gratiæ . And then againe ,
Recordare Iesu pie , and the
like . Which he pronoun-
ced, with so cleare a voyce ,
so constant a memory , and
with a countenance so se-
rene, that all such as were
present (himselfe only ex-
cepted) did weep outright.
Which he obseruing , and
making silence , and taking
his own face into his hands,
he stood still a whyle , in
mentall prayer . And then
turning towardes me , he
sayd ; *Confiteor* (b) *Deo Omni-*
potenti , & tibi Pater . I accuse

O 2   *my*

(b) The
entrance
wherby,
we be-
gin to
make our
Confessiō.

my selfe of this , and this , and
that ; I deo (c) *precor &c.*

And then, inftantly he
added this : *Father, I would
defire* (d) *this laft fauour of you;
that you would confeffe me at
the blocke ; and that, whyleft I,
on the one fide, with my beades
in my hand, might fay* , O bone Iefu , fis mihi Iefus ; O
good Lord Iefus, be thou a
Iefus to me ; *and you on the o-
ther* , Ego te abfoluo &c . I
abfolue thee &c . *at the fame
inftant , the iron might fall vpon my necke* . Not fo , my
Lord, fayd I. For fo , by
giuing

(c) This
we vfe to
fay when
we haue
ended it.

(d) A far
greater
matter it
was to
aske this
fuite ,
then to
grant it.

giuing a figne to the executioner for the cuttinge off
your head, I should becom
(e) *Irregular*. No, no, I will
not doe it, by any meanes.
But then, obferuing that he
was much afflicted, by my
negatiue, and fo rather to
quiet him, then for any
thing elfe, I fayd it might
perhappes be thus, better
done. You may *confeffe* at
the blocke; and being con-
feffed, you may begin to inuoke

(e) By the *Canons* of the holy Church, a Prieft may not cooperat to the death of any man though neuer fo far off; but only for the punifh-ment of delin-quents in courfe of Iufti-ce ; nor then nei-ther, but

O 3

with particuler difpenfation, and that in very rare cafes ; The *Inquifition* hath nothing to do heerin, but only examineth, and leaueth fuch as are faulty and impenitent to the fecular Iudges.

,, uoke the name of *Iesus* ; and
,, when I shall fee, that the
,, Executioner is ready to let
,, downe the iron, I may fay
,, with a lowd voice, *Ego te ab-*
,, *foluo* &*c*. Yet perhapps a-
,, gaine, this would be more
,, inconuenient; for by giuing
,, you a figne, of when the
,, iron were vpon the point of
,, falling, it might fright you
,, in fuch fort, as that, if by
,, the motion of your body, it
,, should not fall iuft vpon
,, you, it would mangle you,
,, and fo afflict you, with a
,, double paine, and a double
death.

death. I will not do it, by »
any meanes. »

At thefe words, cafting
his head vpon my bofome,
he fayd; *Ah Father, euen by*
all that loue which you beare to
this miferable finnefull foule, do
me this fauour. I make a pro-
mife to you, in the name, and
by the help of God, that you fhal
not put me into terrour by it.
For Gods loue belieue me; I be-
feech you giue me credit. Wher-
upon yet, I continuing, as
I had refolued before; *O God*
(fayd he) *and might not thy*
diuine Maiefty, mooue the hart

O 4   *of*

*of this my Father, to esteeme me
worthy of this fauour?* Well,
be of courage (sayd I, to
quiet him) I promise you,
that I will do it. *Then giue
me* (answered he) *that* (f) *sacred hand of yours*. And I
gaue it to him, with this
purpose, that if he should
not remember it at the
blocke, as I verily thought
that he would not, then I
would let it passe; and that
if he remembred it, and did
franckly call for it, I would
performe it. But it seemed
(as I said) to me, that a man
could

(f) The
handes
of Ca-
tholike
Priests,
are an-
noynted
and con-
secrated
with
great so-
lemnity.

could hardly be of fo vn-
daunted a mind; as that, in
fo hard a paſſage , his memory would ſerue him tor
ſuch a buſines ; and that,
wheras àll men procure to
diuert their mind frō ſuch a
blow, this *Barō* would needs
haue an expreſſe ſigne therof. But , in fine , where the
grace of God doth enter , it
produceth effects , which
do farre out-ſtripp all the
power of nature ; and no wit
of man arriueth to them.

When I had made him
this promiſe; *I* (g) *would know*

O 5   (ſayd

(g) His
hart
wrought
mightily
towards
humility

(said he) *whether your* Reuerence, *will not thincke it fit* ,
*that I giue thankes , and de-
mand pardon, of them who haue
had most to do with me , in this
place.* I told him, that I liked
well of it; and hauing giuen
him *Absolution* , I intreated
him by a signe, to sit downe.
Then he said ; *Father , take
you the care of my iourney from
hence to the blocke , as you haue
already promised ; and you shall
go aduertising me , from pace to
pace , of such thinges as are fit ,
that I may haue, my whole soule
for God alone.* I will aduertise
                              you

you , (said I) of all ; Keep »
your selfe prepared , and sit »
downe . »

As soone as he was set ,
all the stringes of our very
harts , seemed to be moued
at once,to pray him that he
would be mindfull of vs in
heauen . And (h) euery one (h) It is
of vs who were preset, both that
with wordes , and tears, did they saw
recōmend himselfe to him, tokens
the best he could; and we fauour
were not able to satisfie our in him:
selues , in the desire we had
of expressing kindnes to-
wardes him . And verily ,
                              this

this was a death, of so much tendernes, that the remembrance of it at this time, doth affect me, at the very soule. Only the yong Noble Man, remained with a most Angelicall Countenance; and with a hart which seemed, not so much as to know, what belonged to feare.

This (i) *Signor Troilo*, was tal of stature; of delicate constitution; of colour rather oliuaster, then very faire; of black haire & thick; of face, neither fatte, nor leane

(i) A description of *Signor Troilo's* person, and fashion.

leane; his eyes were blacke,
and full, and quicke; his
nofe fweetely raifed; his
mouth of a iuft proportion,
& rather fmiling, thé other
wife; his forhead competét-
ly fpatious, & he had not
fo much as one fingle haire
vpon his cheekes. Of a
fweete voice, of ready anfweares; & fo complete in
good fashion, that euen at
the block, he failed not to
falute, & refalute all men,
according to the occafion,
& their condition; and not
being able to take of his hat
him-

himselfe, to make others do
it for him. It hapned once
that I desired him to let me
wipe his face with a hand-
hercheife; not that he was
in any sweate, but only to
refresh him a little. But he,
hauing suffered me, to begin to do him that seruice,
sayd; *Father, I need not this.*
But I desired, that at least
he would rub his face with
his own hands, for it would
refresh him; and instantly
doing so, he said, to me
in myne eare; *Father, I had
an extreame desire, to stretch
my*

my selfe, but me thought, it had somewhat of the Clowne.

In conclusion, he caused all those souldiars who had kept guard ouer him, to passe before him, one, by one; and so, (k) casting himselfe vpon his knees, to euery one of them, as they singly passed, he asked pardon, most humbly of them, with Noble and Christian wordes; and he left them also, liberall donatiues. To the Gentleman *Porter*, he did the like, and more, excusing himself

(k) It is a true signe, & a certain fruite of true pennance, to submit a mans selfe mightily for Gods sake.

for

for the trouble which he had giuen him .

But now there remained no more to be done, for the time was run out , whē the (l) *Aue Maria* bell , did found . Vpon the hearing whereof , we al recited that prayer , and he faid it alfo, vpon his knees. Then faluting all the company , he fate down, & was filent. And whileft he held his peace , we fpake amongſt our

(l) In thoſe Countryes there ringeth a bell euery morning, noone, & night, when all men recite 3 . ſhort prayers, in remébrance of the Incarnation of Chriſt our Lord . This they do wherefoeuer they be , when the bell ringes, though it be in the ſtreets ; and there they ſalute one another , with a wiſh of the good day, or night ,

our felues , with aftonish-
mét at many things, which
we had obferued in him, &
they were thefe . He did neuer fweate . He neuer com-
playned of any thing . He
neuer placed himfelfe, with
any shew of wearines vpon
his chaire He neuer shewed any vnquietnes . He neuer wept , but whyleft he
was making his confeffion .
He neuer fought to eafe
himfelfe , in the courfe of
Nature. He neuer had any
thirft . He neuer fainted .
He was neuer fleepy . He
　　　P　　　　was

was neuer ouerwroght with forrow. He was euer fresh, and strong, hauing been, in that night, fo many, and many tymes vpō his knees. He euer anfwered readily, and with a liuely voice. His memory neuer failed, or fo much as wauered. He was handfomely, and modeſtly apparelled. He (m) fpake not fo much as an inconfiderate word. He neuer expreſſed a defire of any thing. He had, at certayne tymes, and vpon certaine occaſions, a difcharged, and fmiling

(m) A ſtrange image of perfection, was this yonge Noble Man.

ſmiling countenance . He
did completely giue euery
man thoſe titles of reſpect ,
which was his due; without
fayling ſo much as once; as
to one , of *Reuerence* , to another, of *Honour*; to another
of *You*. He declared, moſt
currantly , his laſt *VVill* ,
which was, a sheet of paper,
long . He was not taken by
paſſionate tendernes, but
only vpon the ſpeach of the
Lady his Mother. He ſpake
moſt honourably , & chri-
ſtianly, of the Prince, & of
the Iudges; yea and euen of

them

them, who profecuted the cauſe againſt him . All which particulers, or the moſt part of them, do happen otherwiſe, in others, who are ſubiect to the like condition. So that all thoſe old experiéced *Confortatori* of that *Congregation*, which is called of the *Miſericordia*, were amazed, to ſee how aboundantly the Grace of God, had wrought vpon that ſoule, in the ſpace of a few houres .

When this moſt deuout Noble Man, had thus held
his

his peace, and we had been difcourfing, amongft our felues, of the thinges afore-fayd, he calling me towards him, who yet was ftanding not farre off, fpake to me, in this manner. *Deare Father, let vs make our laft Reconciliation with God.* And then he made a short recapitulation, of all his faults; and began (n) to accufe himfelf, of thinges fo extreamely fmall; as hath giuen occafion, & matter to this foule of myne, vntill this day, wherein I write, and will,

(n) A happy foule to be fo fpeedily, and fo intierly cleanfed.

P 3   vntill

vntil the houre of my death, both to be comforted, and confounded.

Being vpon the end of his Confession, he fell into a most ardent weeping; in such sort, as that bowing downe his head towards my hand, I was not able to endure the heat of his breath. And when I sayd to him, " *Troylo* my Sonne ; Cast a " bridle vpon those teares of " yours ; doe not exasperate " your own wound; it is now " inough, and againe inough; " you haue wept inough; you

<u>will</u>

wi'l haue tyme to weep yet „
againe, when you come to »
lay your Head vpon the »
blocke, for (o) Chriſt. His »
anſwere was this; *I haue al-*
ready told you Father, and now
I tell you ſo once againe; I weep
for my ſinnes, and not for my
death. And when your Reuerence *ſhall haue giuen me* Abſolution, *and I ſhall haue per-*
formed the Pennance, *which*
you will impoſe (which only de-
ſerues to be accompanyed with
tears) you ſhall find, that I will
weep no more. And iuſt ſo it
hapned; for wiping his face
P 4 when

(o) He was to ſuffer death for his miſdeds, but he was to beare it patiently and willingly, for the loue of Chriſt

when I had *abſolued* him, &
I hauing acquainted him,
with ſome neceſſityes of
myne owne, to the end that
he might giue me (p) aſſi-
ſtance, in the ſight of our
Lord ; he remayned , with
eyes as full of ſerenity, and
as voyd of teares, as if, in
all his life, he had neuer
wept.

(p) By
this holy
prayers
in hea-
uen.

But then hauing raiſed
himſelfe, it was thought fit,
by all the Company , that
certaine *Pſalmes* should be
repeated , whereof , I was
to põder ſome of the verſes,
togea-

togeather with the *Confor-tatori*; till such time, as his houre should ariue. Wher-upon he sayd, *It is now broade day, and there cannot be much time remayning. Our (q) Lord be bleßed, for making me passe through this night, so happily, and so holily. I thanke you deare Father, & you Gentlemen, for your so greate fauour. The good God reward you for it.* And heere, all of vs recommending our sel-ues againe to his prayers, we also againe beganne the Psalmes.

(q) Great piety & gratitu-de.

P 5   At

At this time, the *Execu-
tioner* came in, and no
man had the hart to tell
him of it; but he perceiuing
that there was a preſſe of
people, did gently turne
his face about, and ſaw him,
As ſoone as he had ſet eye
vpon him, he was not troubled with it at all; but (r) he
armed himſelfe only with
the ſigne of the *Holy Croſſe*;
and making a countenance
to me, who ſtood cloſe by
him, he roſe, and ſayd :
*VVell, the houre is come ; Gen-
tlemen, let vs goe, and that
cheere-*

(r) Vn-
daunted,
holy
courage.

cheerefully. And they all an-
fwearing thus : Yea let it »
be done cheerefully , *Signor* «
Troilo , cherefully , for the »
loue of *Iefus* ; he turned
towardes the *Executioner* ,
who kneeling down at his
feete , to aske his pardon ;
Do your office (faid he) *in the*
name of God , *for fo* , *he will*
haue it. Your Lordship (faid
he) is to vnbutton your
doublet, about your necke.
And he (being as ready on
the one fide , as he was
modeft on the other) with
his owne hands began to
                    vnbut-

« vnbutton. It is not inough,
« said the chiefe *Executioner* ;
« the doublet muſt be put
« off . But the reſt of thoſe
Officers of *Iuſtice* , were not
deſyrous , that he should
put of his doublet . Yet the
generous Noble Man ſaid ,
That howſoeuer, he would do it,
if they thought it fit .For (ſaid
he) *it shall not greatly trouble*
me; and if you haue a mind to it,
I will ſtrippe my ſelfe , from
head to foot, for the loue of God.
Already therefore , he was
beginning to vntye himſelf;
but it ſufficed that he was
vn-

vnbuttoned to the shoulders. Then, one of the *Confortatori* putting him in mind, of *Non erubescam &c.* and the *Officer* comming to tye his arms, in such a fashion, as that, when he should be arriued at the blocke, his body might not haue much leaue to mooue; *In the name of God (sayth he) bind both my armes, and my handes too, if your will be such. For* (s) *my Lord Iesus, was yet, much worse bound for me.*

Being therfore thus accommodated, they cast a gowne

(s) This man had truefaith in Christ our Lord, & his sacred Passion, who in contemplation and imitation thereof, was so willing to suffer, as you see.

gowne about his backe; and he kneeled downe, before the *Altar*; in act, as if he had craued a benediction, at the handes of our Lord. And, without the least change of colour, beginning the *Miserere*, of himselfe; and being come as far as the outward roome, he paused there, with an incredible decency, and grace. And he sayd, to some of the by-standers, *Might I not thanke my Lord, the Gouernour of the Castle, before I dye?* And they, presenting I knowe

not

not what excuſe, of his not
being riſen , he accepted
thereof; and commanded a
Gentleman, who ſerued the
Gouernour , that he should
thanke him in his name .
And hauing demanded par-
don of many of the Aſſi-
ſtants , & exhorting them
in ſome very few wordes to
vertue ; by the example ,
which there they had before
their eyes of the contrary ,
he went on with the very
ſame verſe of the *Miſerere* ,
where he had left before .
And ſometymes , turning
towards

towardes me, he would be saying, *Come* (t) *Father, come; to heauen, to heauen*. And it was a ſtrang thing, that he being in pantoſles, & going downe ſuch a long paire of ſtaiers, as that is; (which ſtayers are much broken by reaſon of the Artillery, which vpon frequēt occaſions, is drawne vp & downe by that way) yet did not his foot once ſlipp. Nay, & I, failing to tread right many tymes, though I were in ſhoos, he willed me to take care of my ſelfe.

When

(t) See whether this Baron were afraid of death or no.

When he was arriued
to the other open ftayres,
where many perfons of the
Caſtle were to fee him; one of
the *Confortatori*, who was
well experienced in thofe
occafions, and ftood on the
one hand, placing a *Crucifixe*
before him (and as it were
couering him therewith)
cryed out, with a ftronge
voice, *Let* (u) *Chriſt Ieſus*
liue; be not frighted, my
Lord. To which he, (after
he had ended the Verfe,
which he was pronoũcing)
made this anfweare ; *Yea*,

(u) *Viua*
Gieſu
Chriſto.

Q   *leſ*

*let Chrift Iefus liue; in whome,
whilft I am hoping, I do not
feare to be confounded.* And
then faid I, *In te Domine
fperaui, non confundar in æter-
num;* which being repeated
by him, he fpake thus to
them; *Take* (x) *the* Crucifixe
*afide; let all the people fee me.
For if I be good for nothing els,
at leaft I may ferue them, for
an example.* There paffed
one that way, with a bottle
of wine in his hand, who
faluted the *Baron,* vpon his
knee, and the *Baron,* cour-
teoufly refaluted him; and
                          fo

(x) A
noble
courage.

so returned to the same
verse of the *Psalme*, which
he had formerly begunne.
Soone after, passing throgh
the people, which stoode
there, a little, thicke, he
sayd; *Learne* (y) *by my exam-*
ple, to liue well, and pray for
me. And thus with *Psalmes,*
& *Iaculatory prayers*, he came
to the blocke, where there
was store of lookers on.

The intrepide *Baron*
pausing there, sayd thus. *I*
would desire, in these last mo-
ments of my life, to see, at least,
and salute, & thanke, the Lieu-

(y) Few
wordes,
and well
chosen.
It is not
there the
fashion,
for a
man to
stand
prea-
ching, at
the place
of his
executi-
on.

Q 2   *tenant*

tenant Gouernour *of the Caſtle, ſince I cannot ſee my Lord, the* Gouernour. But the *Lieutenant*, by no means reſoluing to go towardes him (for the extreme tendernes, wherewith he was taken) the Noble Youth, perceauing it, and turning to me, ſayd; *Father, his hart ſerueth him not to come; and perhaps I make the people ſtay too longe.* O moſt valiant, & moſt vndaunted mind, which was troubled more with the ſleight incommodity of others, then with the apprehenſion of

                his

his owne imminent death.
At laſt, he cheerefully ad-
uauncing forward, the *Lieu-*
tenant, came before him; &
the *Baron*, caſting himſelfe
vpon his knee, ſaid to me,
In courteſy, Father, take off my
hat. Which the good Gentleman obſeruing, *(z)* did , (z) A
with a moſt bitter, & lowd kind cõ-
crye of teares, euen ſpread who
himſelf, all vpõ the groũd; moſt
and the by-ſtanders, vpon exceed
that occaſion, did caſt thé- teſy.
ſelues all, vpon their knees;
nor was there any thing
heard, but a loud voice of
Q 3   teares.

teares This generous yong
Lord, fayd thē, thus to him.
Syr, do not weepe; I had no de-
figne, but to falute you; to thank
you; and to begge your pardon;
as now I do, both of your felfe,
and, in your perfon, at the hands
of al them, who are prefent heer;
defiring them to learne at my coft,
and to pray for my foule. This
he fayd, with fo ftronge a
voice, as that he was heard,
notwithftanding the noife
of their weeping. I alfo, was
not able to ftay my teares;
when he leaning towardes
myne eare, fpake thefe very
wordes

wordes, now below, as before he had done, aboue: *Behould, your Reuerence is weeping; and yet still you tell me, that I must haue a Noble Hart.* Then hauing repeated, diuers times, *In manus tuas Domine, commendo spiritum meum;* and, *Suscipe me Domine, secundum eloquium tuum, & non confundas me ab expectatione mea;* he was wished to ascend and then to lay himselfe downe vpon the Scaffold. At the same instant, one of the *Confortatori* saying to him, *Cheerefully Signor Troi-*

Q 4   *lo,*

lo, *couragiously Signor Troilo*; and a whole crye of prayers being raiſed, and made by all the company for him; that valiant Hart, did anſwere euen with a ſmiling countenance; *Know* (a) *Gentlemen, that I dye cheerefully, for the* Loue *of* Ieſus Chriſt, *& in* Pennance *for my ſinnes*.

(a) A noble, and holy, valiant hart.

　As therefore he was laying down his head; *where* (ſaid he) *is the Father?* And turning towards the *Executioner*, he ſayd, *Stay a whyle; for I will be reconciled*. And beckning me, firſt, towards
　　　　　　　him

him with his countenance;
*Father (sayd he) on this hand,
I place my* (b) Good Angell;
and on that , S. Paul, *and* S.
Iohn the Baptist ; *our* B.
Lady, *shall stand before. Your
Reuerence must remēber, to performe the promise , which you
made me . I will say* , O bone
Iesu, esto mihi Iesus ; *O good
Lord Iesus* , *be thou* a Iesus *to
me; and when you shall see, that
the corde is in cutting, you must
say,* Ego te absoluo &c . *that
so, when I shall inuoke the name
of* Iesus; *and you* absolue me ;
my soule may begin her iourney,

(b) These Saints he vsed, as interces- sours for him to Christ our Lord.

Q 5   *from*

from this body of myne, towards
heaue, by the mercy of my Lord,
as I confide it shall.

I do ingenuously con-
fesse, that I was so mightily
amazed within my selfe, &
I fell into such an excesse of
weeping, that I had not a
word to answere, at the instant, but in the language
of teares. And he, in laying
his head vpon the blocke,
expresly spake these very
wordes : *Deare Father, draw*
neere me. Let it suffice, and I
take you to witnes, That (c) *I*
protest my selfe, in my desire to
lay

(c) So
that his
memo-
ry and
courage
was far
from
fayling
him ; &
perhaps
there is
hardly
to be
found in
any hi-
story, a
nobler
Chara-
cter, of
wisdom,
presence
of mind,
magna-
nimity,
and san-
ctity .

lay downe a thousand heads, in this one head of myne; and in this one life, to offer up a thousand liues. I accuse my selfe, for not doing it, with that feruour of deuotion; that vehemency of Contrition; and that promptitude of resignation, which I haue beene told, and taught. But I know not how to do more. I accuse my selfe, as truly, of all the sinnes, which I haue confessed vnto your Reuerence, as if now I did repeate them to you, one, by one. In Pennance, *if it please you, I will giue my head to* Christ, *as a punishment which*

is

is most deserued by me ; and of you I desire Absolution .

So did this Noble hart, which neither was, nor was to be conquered, or daunted, lay downe that head, vpon the blocke . And saying then , *Bring* (d) *hither the* Crucifixe, *that I may see it ;* he began also to say , *O bone Iesu , sis mihi Iesus ; O good Lord Iesus , be a Iesus to me ,* being accompanyed by all the people , who were already vpon their knees , and who also, inuoked the name of *Iesus .* And my self, standing

(d) See how this true Christiã courage, cõtinues euen to the end, and in the end .

ding

ding clofe, at the one fide of his head, and looking ftill, when the *Executioner* would go about to cut the corde, as foone as I faw, that the knife was lifted vp, for that purpofe, I faid out-right, *Ego* (e) *te abfoluo ab omnibus peccatis tuis, in nomine Patris, & Filij, & Spiritus Sancti, Amen*. He did then, both more fpeedily, and more lowdly then was his cuftome, fay, *Iefu, fis mihi Iefus; O Iefus, be thou a Iefus to me*. And at the inftat, his head flew off, at once, from

(e) I abfolue thee frō all thy finnes in the name of the Father, & of the Sonne, and of the holy Ghoft.

from his body . And my
felfe, with many others alfo,
did fee , that his head being
already cut off, did produce
the laft fyllable of the name
of *Iefus* , with a ftrong kind
of hiffe , or whifper . And
the foule, I truft, did fly vp
free, into (f) Heauen; ador-
ning all his former life ,
with a holy end; vpon that
very day, of the yeare, wher-
vpon the moft Illuftrious
Lord his Father , had de-
parted out of this life, before this Sonne of his was
borne

(f) His
body
was in-
terred ,
in the
*Chiefa
Nuoua* .

borne ; that former being
the 18. of *April, Anno Domini*
1574.

FINIS.

GUILLAUME DU VAIR
Holy Philosophy
1636

HOLY PHILOSOPHY

BY THE R. F.

VVILLIAM

VAIR BISHOP

OF LIZIEVX, AND LORD

KEEPER OF THE GREAT SEALE OF FRANCE,

Wherein briefly and elegantly is expreſſed man's true happines and felicitye.

Tranſlated out of French By J. H.

ANNO M. DC. XXXVI.

APPROBATIO.

HIc libellus de *Sacra Philosophia* nihil co tinet fidei aut bonis moribus contrarium. Actum Duaci 29. Augu. 1636.

Georgius Colvenerius S. Theol. Doct.
& Regius ordinariusae Professor, &
Duacens. Academiæ Cancellarius, &
Librorum Censor.

TO
THE RIGHT
HONOVRABLE
THE LADY
ELIZABETH
Viscontesse Sauage dowager.

ADAME
I most
humbly bow in
this my offe-
ring vpp vnto
your Honour
so small

* 2

ſo ſmall a piece, as weighing with
my ſelf, that a large volume doth
beſt be ſuite a Lady of your excellency . Yet few words oftentimes
(RIGHT NOBLE) com-
priſe| in them great worth, much
ſubſtance, and ſingular grace.

This treatiſe might really be
enſtyled a Compendium or ſum-
mary of pious conſiderations , in-
ſtructions, well ordered and emi-
nent rules. It was formerly deliuered out of French, it's natiue language into Italian, and voted to
the famous CHRISTIANA
daughter of Lorraine great Dut-
cheſſe of TVSCANY, a Lady
& Princeſſe of rare guiftes, deuout,
yea, and who arriued to great perfection.

fection. As that was truely due to her Excellency there, euen so is this here to your Honour, whose addictions to vertue haue so disposed you, yea haue taken such place with you, that you dayly haue gott ground thereof euen so much as you haue arriued to a singular state of perfection, which briefely is of such condition, & such nature as that it euermore earnestly promooueth to conceiue, yet more by dayly contemplations, the fruite whereof produceth a further pious practise.

Yet MADAME I humbly craue you digne to pardō the style of a rude pen. The Author with vnmatchable harmony, admirable sueetnes, euen to the charming of the perufer coutcheth

cheth, yea ſpinneth his fine webb, his
ſound, moſt curious and accurate no-
tions: By me here alas! will this
worke be much leſſened, be impoue-
rished and made weake, as depriued
of it's true luſter with which in it
ſelfe it shineth and equalizeth in my
iudgmēt any whoſoeuer hath at any
time wrote in this language, rare I
ſay whoſoeuer hee bee.

Notwithſtanding let your Honor
regard the trueth of my deliuery of
the Author's ſenſe, and propitiouſly
conniue at my defeĉts and wants in
eloquence, and in ſuch like manner of
expreſſions, which are, & cōdignely
are acknowledged to be inſtruments
to winne more attention, and hence
more impreſſion in the minde. I con-
ſide

fide that the rather I shall acquire
your indulgency herein for that I
may well prefume, that your excellent fpirit will well apprehend the
Authors meaning without that it be
further embellished by fome any
whofoeuer, his more fuch like happy
pen.

Your Honours humbly
deuoted feruant

IOHN HAWKINS,

ERRATA.

P Ag. 26. l.11. read, might enioy. pag. 29. l.
16. read, perceaue all the eff cts. pag. 38. l.
16. read, The species and forme. pag. 56. l. vlt.
read, to frame, and rayse a, &c. pag. 68. li. 2.
read, They dy to Beatitude, they aye to sempi-
ternall happine, of which, etc. pag. 80. l. 7, read,
hath giuen power. pag. 101. l. 10. Ether read,
Non-temperance, or take (in) negatiuely. pa.
103. li. 12. read, which haue also recommended.
pag. 112. l. 6. read, fall out in ingenuous. pag.
172. li. 17. read, instand of affection, disposition
by which. pag. 194. li 14. read, to be the author.
pag. 198. li. 14. read, comprehend not that in
the life.

    In this contemplation, &c.

OF HOLY

PHILOSOPHY.

 EE pro-
perlie re-
femble, and
are much
like vnto
them, who
being in their very greene &
tender youth led captives,
alas! taken prifoners and carried away to fome for aine &
farre remote places, loofe in
the courfe of time, the me-
A   mory

mory of their owne coūtrey,
the vſe of their language, and
the amitv, love & correſpon-
dence of their parents . For
even ſcarce are wee out of our
cradles, but that peruerſe affections vntoward inclina-
tions, and violent windes, doe
ſurpriſe, and filling the ſailles
of our deſires with a thouſand
pleaſing gales of winde blaſts,
doe make vs wander and depart farre from our proper
nature, and eſtrang vs from
true reaſon.

'This litle time, that our
ſoule remaineth in this exile,
in this banishment, it forget-
teth it's beginning, looſeth
the remembrance of it's well-
being,

being, and it's good estate
and what is found at length
worse, it's knowledg of it's
selfe. Oh! were we at least altogether like vnto thole captives, thole poore slaues. For
if after a long captiuity there
be hope givé them of returne,
or that they but onely heare
of their natiue Countrey; you
shall see them leape for ioy,
so much comfort apprehend
they of this newes. Wee con-
trarywise haue nothing that
displeaseth vs more, thē thole
who remember vs, put vs in
minde of our first state and
being, and we abhorre no-
thinge more then the tracts
which chalketh out our way,

A 2   which

which evidently demonstra-
te's vnto vs what courfe vve
ought to runne . Thefe fuch
like would forfake the fortunate I flands to returne to one
Ithaque affixed as to a neft
on a rough and sharpe rocke:
Nor will wee at all decline,
avoide, or releafe our felves
out of the mire, where wee
hardly breath , for to paffe
into a certaine and perpetuall
felicity . But thou wilt vrge
thus , where is this felicity ?
Shew vnto vs that which we
defire: who is hee would re-
fufe to be happy? Alas! the
word doth pleafe thee , but
thou flyeft the effect it felfe :
at leaft thou art shye, and fol-
                                loweft

lowest but the shadow, in
meane while the body, the
true & reall substance fiyeth
from thee: and hunting after
a vaine cloudy mist of volup-
tuousnes, of sensuality, thou
leauest the proper, true, solid,
and incomparable pleasure.
Where then is it? sayest thou
to me: shew it vs by tracke &
footstepp, that wee may finde
it out, that wee may speedily
arriue there & enioy it Who
would not laugh to scorne
such an one who being bleare-
eyed, who being weake of
sight should intreate and importune *Pilon* to shew his
worke: or who would not

A 3   slight

flight them who are deafe by
catarrhe, by defluxion, who
should ftruggle and crowde
to heare the Mufique of the
great Lord *Baif*? should not
one fay vnto fuch an one, get
ftayed thefe humours which
fall one thine eyes, dazle thē,
yea dimme thy fight; procure
that the humour which hath
made thy hearing thicke be
taken away, be dryed vp;and
then I fay to thee thou shalt
fee our excellent peintures;&
to thee, thou shalt heare our
delicate fonges. Euen as the
fulnes and voluptuoufnes of
the fenfes cannot be vveil ap-
prehended, but by thofe who
                    enjoy

enjoy entire health, who are
found of body and well-dif-
pofed : euen fo the content
and fatisfaction of the fpirit
cannot,where refideth, where
allodgeth the height of our
happines our felicity, I fay,
cannot be clearly perceiued
but by thofe who have pur-
ged, cleanfed their foules of
all thofe difordinate and vitious affections , which like
vnto maligne vlcers extinguish the vitall fpirits even
there where they firft had
their being, where they were
engendred. Looke thé about
thee, marke vvell if fo that
thou be refolued to make thy

felfe

selfe capeable to taſt of the
fruites of this eternall beatitude. Yet giue me leaue, I well
perceiue, that thou ſo nour-
tured even from thy greene
years in the pleaſures which
ſenſe giveth thee, and thou
ſetteſt ſuch valuation, ſuch
eſteeme, ſuch price on them,
thou accountſt thé ſo dearly
deare vnto thee; that thou art
even shaken with feare, thou
even all over trébleſt to leave
them, to departe from them,
if ſo that I give not vnto thee
a gage, a pledge, an earneſt of
that other vnlimited and infinitly ſurpaſſing joy, whereof
I deliver much comfort, yet
                              shewe

shewe not clearly, and give thee fight thereof, but a farre of. But póder vvell. Who is it, that fo able is, that can make evidently appeare to men, who are as yet but earth, the ftate, and difpofition of a pure foule, and innocent, it's perfect actions and all celeftiall, in vvhich confifteth this fupreame contentment, this ioy, and incomparable jewell? To speake plaine in footh you preffe me, you rub me too neere to the quick, & require of mee more then I can performe. Yet not to leave you difgoufted, difcontented and difcouraged I vvill vfe all my

A 5   en-

endeavour . I vvill doe like
vnto them who carry hither
and thither, their sights of
Monsters and such like pro-
digious shewes; they set the
image & protraicture through
out all the fower quarters of
the Towne, yea & at the place
of their being, then after the
shewe the true and naturall
body, when so that the people
haue first payed at the dore,
and that they have taken their
severall places of vewe.

The spectacle, the sight, the
shew to vvhich I inuite you, is
this *Sapience*, which vvell may
be enstyled the trueth , and
knowledge of all things what-
soever

foever, but particulary and principally of divine things; vvhich is replenished vvith clearenes, brightnes, and incredible fplendour; vvhich could vve behold in lively grace and beauty, it vvould even overcome vs vvith love, & vvould vvorke in vs a hate of meane, lovv, and abject terreftriall things, vvherevvith we are fo much poffeft wherevvith wee are fo much carryed away, alas! and defperately loft. I vvill fet herein fome thing like portraitures in high vvayes. If fo that you difpofe your felfe to goe the right way to the gate, you fhall herein

fee

see both the guiding Image,
and follovving advancement,
and comfort vvhich is truely
marveilous. And vvhen you
shall have paied your custome
and passed out of the foule
vvay of this life, you shall behold that vvhich no tongue
can vtter, & no eare câ heare.
But for tó make thee côceive
as it vvere a farre of vvhat
thing this is, and to present
vnto thee some rough casts: I
vvill entreate thee to consider
those things vvhich thou ad-
mirest in this vvorld, and for
obtaining of vvhich thou art
so eager, and active: thou shalt
finde that if thou passest onely
vp

up vvard as vpon steps of stai-
res all vigilant on thy right
vvay, these things shall bring
thee at the end to the knovv-
ledge of that vvhich at the
present thou desirest. But where
as in stead of ascending thou
setlest thy selfe there and res-
test satisfied, thou therein dost
onelie hence abase thy selfe &
becommest foule and nasty.
But let vs novv a litle observe
vvhat is that vvherewith thou
gluttest thy senses, and hence
proceedeth this sloth and this
alluring jewell , on vvhich
thou seate st thy vvorldly felicity. Doth it take it's source,
it's ground, it's foundation, is
it

it peradventure derived from
naturall objects, frō naturall
things vvhich are arrived and
poſſeſſed with certaine perfections? Are they not colours
vvell & curiouſly tempered,
vvell mingled, ſelected, and
aptly ſet before thy view, and
from the proportions, and de-
menſions exactly obſerved,
vvhich give comfort, and
ſprightly ioy to thine eyes!
And vvhat other admireſt
thou in a Meadow enameled,
& all over caſt with a thouſand and thoſe delicate, lively
and ſpecious flowers, in countryes ſo variouſly diuerſified,
curiouſly comparted, & rarely

ly distinguished, in the brave,
sumptuous , and moſt ma-
gnificent buildings of Kings,
in their rings, their jewells, in
their tables of excellent art of
painting : but onelie this curious obſervations? The faire
& gratefull faces of vvoemen,
for vvhich thou ſo weakly o-
vercome , impotêtly burneſt:
vvhat is there in them to be
valiewed, what to be eſteemed
but a ſymmetry, and exaƈt di-
ligence in Nature , a pleaſant
proportiõ in the conformatiõ
and vnion of many different
things? The ſweete of a voice
rarely harmonious , farre ſurpaſſing others, or the melody
of

of many voices vvell according   vvhat haue they other
then a true, and vvell ordered
continuance of times , or an
incounter of many founds ,
anfwereable to the rule and
proportiõ which nature hath
thereon impreffed? The moft
pleafantft and moft fweetly
odoriferous fmells that one
may at any time fmell: vvhat
haue they but a certaine tépe-
rature of heate & moifture, &
a certaine qualitie fixed in a
body through the concurfe
of many caufes . In meates,
though of moft exquifite
tafts there is none fweete, and
vvell pleafing and agreable to
                               the

the palate, but the felfe fame
vvell obferved meafure in
minghing of the liquors: Yea
even the fence of toutching cā
yeild thee no other pleafure
& delight, onelie that therein
vvee finde certaine equalities,
and neate fmoothnes in naturall bodyes. Place before
thy fight and imagination, all
the delights and pleafures in
array, & in the beft equipage
and higheft degree, that thy
fenfes can arriue to. For thefe
onelie thou fpendeft thy life
in defires, for thefe onely thou
toyleft thy felfe, for thefe
onely thou ftrugleft vvith the
impetuous vvindes and com-
                         mitteft

mittest thy selfe to the mercy
of the seas. But if so that each
of these particular things do
stay thee, yea arrest thee, and
ceaie on thee vnder a certaine
vaine & disguised apparance
of beauty, vvhich issueth frō
this such artificial cōposition:
how vvouldest thou be taken,
hovv rapt if so that thou fall
into the consideration of all
their endovvments together
& all att once, from their be-
ginniug to the height of their
perfection: Shouldst thou not
finde the selfe same difference
that is betvveene one onelie
single stone, and a statelie and
most sumptuous Palace, the
                        same

same which is knovvn to be
in one voice, ånd a compleate
concorde, a cópleate Musique
of many? which is vnderstood
betvveene one finger and the
vvhole entire body ? What
accoumpt, alas! what esteeme
what valuation can you attri-
bute to all these particular
things, principally of those
which are of earth , ah! mee-
rely terrestriall : when as looking vp, & advauncing thine
eyes towards the sunne and
starre you shall behold the
words fró the first to the last,
from the even highest to the
lovvest ; and shalt take into
thy consideration, how many
                                    sort

sort of marvailes, and strang
wonders are there deciphered
yea on all sides, & in each part
painted out the life? But if so
that we are to giue repast, and
satisfie our senses onelie, and
to even ouercome them, yea
euen glutt them with the cõ-
municatiõ of those vvhich are
beautifull, and excellent: yet
at least it ought to be this
vvhole and entire vvorke,
the excellentie & perfection
vvhereof consisteth in the relation, and vnion of the other
particular beauties. But our
soule vvhich bravely aduanceth his desires and vvishes to
an higher state then doe the
sences

ſenſes ſaving that vve enthrall
it & ſtifle it through the vio-
lence of our paſſiós litle careth
to ſtay there. It findeth nothing vvhich either will keepe
it, conſerue it, retaine it, or có-
taine it. For it embraceth that
which is of more conſequéce,
and farre more magnificall
then vvhatſoever is ſpoken
of, it comprehendeth aſvvell
héaven, as earth throughout
all the vvorld, the Vniverſe, it
paſſeth to the profunditie, to
the depths of gulphs, bottóles
pitts, knovveth all things,
moveth it ſelfe by his innate
vertue and facultie, and is ſo
excellent, ſo purely rare in it's
ovvne ſelfe: that bee it vve
con-

cóserve in it's naturall beauty
and perfection, all the things
which are found in the vale of
this lavv vvorld would cleerly
appeare by comparison made
to be both deformed & fouly
vgly After it hath conteplated
it selfe, and that it hath employed and exercised it selfe
in the search, and serious in-
quiry of the Causes of things,
and the knovvledg of them;
not finding ought in all that,
no nor in her such being
vvhich may latisfie her, and
settle the desire shee hath to
apprehend and rightly know,
shee is compelled to raise her
selfe vp, and soare above the
vvorld, and her selfe, and to
give

give her selfe over to be conducted by the vvorkes, to the
Workeman There it behol-
deth, there it difcerneth clearly
at once and in one fight all
thinges and all fortes of beauties and perfections vvhat-
foever vvhich properly concerne the groud & fountaine
from vvhence they vvere de-
parted; and they vvh vvere
found more excellent and admirable, they approach more
nigh the place from vvhich
they firft came: No otherwife
thé the beames of the Sunne
vvhich feeme greater, purer,
and brighter, the more nigh
are they to the maine body
vv hich

vvhich fendeth them forth,
and cafteth them fprightlie
here & there promifcuoufly.
Willingly therein do I vfurpe
this comparifon, for that of
all thinges that vvee knovve
in this vale below,there is not
any thinge vvhich hath more
proportion, more fimilitude
to our foule, then our fight,
vvhich is the moft noble, the
moft lively and the quickeft
and readieft action of all our
fenfes. Nor is there any thing
fo like vnto God Almighty as
is Light and fplendour, which
is the refin'dft, pureft, and
moft illuftrious and excellen-
teft thing of the World. In

fo much

fo much as the *Magi*, the auncient wife mē fayed that God
hade a lucide, bright, & tranf-
parant body, & that his foule
vvas all trueth, having herein
delivered vnto vs , and found
by chaunce, and as it vvere to
them in darkenes the greateft
myfteries, one of the greateft
fecrets of diuinitie . It then
cōcerneth our duety, to open
and vnfeale the eyes of our
foule, that wee may penetrate
this diuine light that wee may
finde this light , even to the
profunditie & depth of everlafting trueth . Were it that
vve vvould give but fome
fmall helpe , fet but alas ! a

B   hand

hand in affiftance of our foule
to afcend the ftaires vvhich
are apparát, and ready for vs,
& that we would addreffe her
flight directlie to the height:
vvhat pleafure, what delight
muft not be hoped for, but
wished for; not wished for,
but fpoken of, not fpoken of;
but be confident of; from
whence we might ▬▬ enioy
all plenitude, all fulnes? A
pleafure, an vnexpreffible ioy
whofe increafe yea & redou-
bling vve shalbe fenfible of
vntill that thou mounted vp
to the height, vve shalbe ioyned vvith to the principall, &
more eminentlie bright light.
                              Then

Then all environed, all pof-
feffed by fplendor,& extafed,
traunced vvith the afpect, vi-
fion,contemplation, the fight
of this marvailous and vnexpreffible beautie, vve shall
feele the pleafure the ioy to
multiplie it felfe beyond meafure, to all incomprehenfible
infinitie which vvill replenish
vs vvith vnmatchable heart-
comfort, & in vs vvill worke
fuch an effect, as that vve in-
genioutlie and generoutlie
shall difdaigne and account
at nought vvorth thofe flit-
ting, fading, and corruptible
delights, all it's weeke, fainte
alas! and changeable fweets,
  B 2   which

which we gaze at, and are as it
vvere hence amafed and aftonished at   here in this lovv
vale, and there is nothing that
is worth the vvishing for alas !
but a litle, and fmall (I know
not hovve to terme it) fparkle
of beautie fparingly and nig-
gardly caft on them, given
vnto them. Then fhall vve be
admitted, and enter to the
shopp, where haue beé framed
all thefe rare workes, wee shall
not onely fee the modells, nor
haue the inftruméts by which
in our hands : but alfo vvee
shall perceive, & eafily knovv
the vvorkem an himfelfe. Hee
vvill not onelie shevve vs his
                                 worke ;

worke, nor vvill onelie deci-
pher & point out his defignes,
but he vvill teach vs his heart
and fcience, & hee vvill make
vs fully perfect, and altogether divine like vnto himfelf.
There shall vvee clearly fee
the beames, the rayes of his
Divinitie enlarging it felfe
everie vvhere, to the reuni-
ting it felfe to this body of
light, to vvhich vvhen fo that
vvee shalbe once arrived to
by our contemplation, vvee
shall inftantlie perceiue all
~~the caufes and~~ effects of the
everlafting vvifdome vvhich
particularlie and feverallie
might feeme to be of povver

to

to compleatlie furnish our
content . Marke then vvell
the ſtate of our felicitie. It
is to this inexhauſtible fountaine of beautie, to this profound ſea, & depthes of goodnes, that the fourdes & rivers
of the vvorld conduct vs. It is
this originall light to vvhich
vve muſt turne to , and on
which vvee muſt firmelie fixe
the eyes of our ſoules , be it
that vve aime at everiaſting
bleſſing , eternall beatitude.
Ah ! how rare, how excellent
vvas the laſt breath, the laſt
vvordes of that greate Philo-
ſopher *Plotin* vvho hauing his
ſoule evé thé departing fró his
                    body,

body,vvould that his scholers should be called together,they there being preseut he delivered vnto them these his last vvordes. Happines attend yee alvvaies my freinds, and to be such convert that vvhich you haue of divine impressed in you to the first and highest divinitie. O generous speeeh! and vvorthy to be the last, & to be delivered at the end of the life of a Philosopher! But what is it that vve shall doe to returne vnto God, how shall we behaue our selves sound & vvhole vvith him, that vve may arriue to such felicitie?
Shall vve be so bold as to pre-
sent

ſēt our ſelues in that ſuch our
ſtate vve are in ordinarilie? ve-
rilie, no, for if ſo that before
vve lift vp the eyes of our
ſoule towards this clearlie
bright and faire irradiating
ſparkling light , vve cleanſe
not our ſelues, doe not puriſy
our ſelues in liew of enioying,
poſſeſſing of it's beautifull &
pure ſplendor, that our ſight
vvith vvhich vve in ſuch ſmall
portion were endowed vvith,
will be dimmed, alas! quite ex-
tinguished. For even as in the
law of the *Iewes*, the woeman
vvho came to the proofe ,
the tryall of the ſacrifice of
jealouſie , if ſo it were that
she

she were chaft, entire and in-
corrupt shee was not ought
prejudiced by that myfteriall
water, but paffed from that
water without blame, yea or
any fufpition whatfoever, cō-
trariwife had shee violated
her conjugall, her matrimo-
niall faith shee appeared infected, shee putrified & brake
in funder. Euen fo they who
like members of the Church
of God haue maried his
onely Sonne, if fo that they
prefent themfelues polluted,
contaminated and fpotted,
to touch the pure and facred
fire of his holie fpirit ; they
are to be inftyled rather

B 5   blinde

blinde then clearre of sight,
rather consumed; yea, and
reduced into ashes, then
warmed. Héce is it that when
God compassionating our
overthrow, alas! our ruine,
was pleased for our safety to
disclose to the world this light
of Sapience, of vvisdome, of
well distinguishing & iudging,
he fote-sent his Herald to prepare the soules of them vvho
ought and vvould participate
of his grace, take hold thereof, and contemplate the splé-
dour of his glorie. One might
well heare to resoúd throughout the Vniverse the Saintly
voice of that Prophet thus
crying

crying out: make plaine, make
even the waies of the living
God, doe pennance, and produce fruites worthy of your
repentance; for he will come
vvith a winnowing five in his
hand to fever the corne apart
from the ftraw and to caft the
ftraw into an vnquenchable
fire. Since then that fo it is
that wee defire this felicitie,
this greate happines, and that
before we prefent our felues
it is expedient, nay apparantly
neceflarie that we purifie our
fpirits, & make them capable
to receiue diuine things. Let
vs well obferve what reme-
dies, what meanes, what waies
wee

wee haue apt & fit to obtaine
such an effect , to arriue to
such an end . But first let vs
consider a while how so it cō-
meth to passe that we are so fou
le; to the end that vve may the
more knovv vvhat is most
proper, most fit to cleanse vs :
let vs see from vvhence ,
and by vvhich vvay vve are
fallen ; that vvee may vnderstand the meanes to releiue &
recouer our selues . God Almighty savv nothing in all
other his vvorkes which came
nigh , vvhich approach to his
perfection; he savv them farre
& farre belovv his perfection;
he had a vvill, & euen then re-
salued

solued as for his cheife vvorke
and maifter-piece to mould,
yea and figure himfelfe and
make his onne fimilitude, to
produce to the world a liuing
Image of his Diuinity. Oh!
but what was the iffue thereof? Man incontinently appeared on the face of the earth,
fo perfect and accomplished
that nothing elfe could be fur
ther defired, fo compleate to
whō nothing could be added.
For this image drawn to the
life, & hauing in it, as is feene
in a picture, many draughts
abbreuiated and drawn in
fmall cōpas many lines, many
cafts of the aire contenance &

prin·

principall grace of the subject
was in it's perfection truelie
aboue marvaile. The sacred
fire vvhich God inspired into
him being most pure, made
his vnderstanding cleare and
replenished him vvith the
knowledg of all things. In
such sort that hauing trueth
for guide, and vertue for help,
all his actions vvere conformable to reason: and being
alwaies turned to his Creator
receiveth in himselfe a pure
chriftall or well polished looking-glasse the species and
forme of the Divinitie: in the
Contemplation vvhereof hee
fixed and setled his thoughts,

and

and all his defires, and hence
vvas he became very happy;
for he lived in God, and God
in him. But this looking-
glaſſe which vvas ſo enabled,
endowed, poliſhed, and beau-
tified by meanes of the object
of the Divinitie, being now
turned avvay from thence, &
all bent to follow ſmoke,
miſts, and foggs, is become
duskish, hath loſt his luſter &
is miſerablie ſoyled : inſo-
much as hece this immortall
brightnes, this glorious ſplendor diſdaigning to preſent it
ſelfe and import it ſelfe, and
hath left him, and abandoned
him to obſcurities, and even
                     darkenes

darkenes it selfe. Euen ſa man who before that he reuolted and turned himſelfe away from God, was replenished with a certaine knowledg of all thinges is now become as one foule, & in him both error and lyes haue taken the place of verity, of trueth, & earneſt fiery and vmbridled concupiſcence, filthy deſire hath the place and ſeate of a well gouerned, well tempred, and moderate will: all his thoughts which were attentiue and v-nited to contemplate the Creatour, are now employed and caſt on the creatures, and without conductor, guide,

                                    or

or reafon at all hazard care-
lefly haue wandred : this
ardent côcupifcency thus ex-
pofed and laid open, hath immediately enrertained finne,
the which arriued to full encreafe, hath procured & drawn
on death . Death truely the
grearest euill and vttermoft
of all euills . Death that
height of horrour , and ob-
fcurity, of blacke and affrigh-
ting darkenes wherewith fo
long as a man is enuironed,
alas! euery vay incompaffed,
it is not in his power to receiue the fplendor & biight-
shining beanes of immortall
light, & to reafume the guide
of

of trueth, whose onely object
and aspect is of ability to retaine & continue him, in the
state of felicitie. Man beholding such his case, that hee
was come to such a being, &
in such manner disfigured, &
disguised, was dis usted, dis-
pleased at himselfe, yea irk-
some to himselfe, and even to
execrating, to cursing his led
life as a gulph of miserie,
wherein nothing was presented to his eyes, to his veiw,
but darknes and confusion.
All his designes were no other
then evill, all his hopes, but
calamities; for that God being
all iust, and man the height
of

of sinne , what measure or what end ought he to expect, and haue in his sufferance, & punishment? But the ever-lasting & vncreated Sapience, the eternall Wisdome, who had wrought with God his Father in the Creatiō of man, taking pitty of the perdition, the losse, and vtter ruine of such a worke, came, as *Tertulian* delivereth, to allay, to ex-tennate, and dissolue the ve-nome of death with his owne blood, to wash, and make vs cleane and pure, & to encline the iust indignation of his Father, to be mercifull vnto vs, and returne to vs. Behold then

then vs returned to grace,
vvith our God, and through
him, marke vvell that by his
mercy, vvee are purified, and
againe called to the knowe-
ledg of his verity, his trueth,
and cotemplation of his glory. But vvee are so vvilfull, &
so giuen ouer to our ovvne
humours, to our losse, & our
vnhappines, and such like eni-
mies of our felicity, that
asooneas this eternall light be
ginneth to shevv it selfe apparantly, and most brightly on
the albe, the table, the blanke,
the looking-glasse of our co-
sciences to expresse, and imprint the face and contenance
of the diuinity; to restore and

make good again: the duskish
& decayed draughts; and as it
were expunged, & blotted out
of this Sapience, this diuine
vvifdome, vvee dravve on our
felues a thoufand impurities,
which dull our fight or thické
it notably, yea blind vs, & in-
terpofe théfelues betvveene
vs, & the grace which illumi-
nateth & should enlighté vs.
Therefore it is expedient, yea
neceffary that as vvee foile our
felues vve haue the ready and
helping hands to cleanfe vs &
make our foules pure, to the
end that they hauing made it
cleare and vvell polished the
beames of the Soueraigne
goodnes

goodnes may shine & fed forth
fprightly gliftering beames,
and clearnes of vertue and the
brightnes of trueth. Now let
vs attend the meanes which
we are to vfe , let vs ponder
well vvhat may be the caufe
of this fo greate an ill, and let
vs vvell confider vvhat reme-
dies are to be aptly applyed.
Our iudgment perverted, yea
and corrupted is the caufe and
fountaine of this our iuft hei-
nous calamity vvhich pefti-
lently doth infect and deftroy
vs . That vvhich efpecially
vndoeth vs and putteth vs
much out of frame , is the
delights and over-vveaninge
pleafures

pleasures vvhich attract vs ,
allure vs on every side, and
make vs sottish , yea drunke
before that vve are avvare,
before that vve are broad
avvake ; for these liquours
being tempred among our
senses, as yet tender in the de-
bility , the vveakenes of our
years, vve so savourly and de-
litiously assay & tast thereof,
that vve can never after recall
our selues into our selues, that
vve can never forget & loose
the tast thereof. Not satisfied
to drinke hereof, vve plunge
and ingulfe our selues therein,
so farre forth, that even as the
flovving of the Sea retireth it
selfe,

selfe , leauing vs at it were
drovvned vpon the coaft and
bāke of miferable old yeares.
But obferue vvell thefe
fvveets vvherevvith greedily
vvee fill our felues , turne immediately to bitternes,filling
our fpirits vvith a venemous
humour with infect them , &
fully corrupteth them . For
the affection we beare to the
beauty of things created
being entertained, and to too
much made of , changeth it
felfe into a furious, outragious
and vmbridled-vvill , vvhich
peruerteth vs and turneth our
fenfes out of all frame:the defire which we haue to worldly
                            ritches

ritches being lulled and dif-
gnifed. doth conuert it felfe
into a blind and fenceleffe
paffion to efteeme to value in
this world nothing more then
the filth and excrement of
the earth: the loue of a fee-
ming shadowed and falfe honour is couerted into a fimple
defire to be greater then
others of the world, and to
appropriate and challeng to
himfelfe the reuerence, ducty
and feruice which is due to
G o d onely: the pleafure
which we take in our nou-
rishment is conuerted and
changed into a brutish and
infamous gurmandizing and

C　　　　fordid

fordid gluttony: the care we
take to conferue our bodyes
delicately, is no other then a
remiffenes, drowfines, watch-
lefnes: and the fire by which
we giue confidence to of our
courage is, cháged into infó-
lency, and an outragious
choler, moodines, & rashnes.
Certainely our fpirits oppref-
fed, shut vp, and notably
hindred by fo vitious, & fuch
entangling birdlime like humours, are not of ability to
breath ought that pure is, and
truely neate & cleane. Well,
now to releafe, to purge all
thefe the fubtill wily and
mortall poifons and paffions
of

of the spirit, it is expedient
that wee serioufly attend to
the difcouery of fome remedy
which may be auaileable, and
well may it be aduifed and
much to our purpofe to take
the counfaile which a good
auncient father gaue his young
fcholler and nouice. Euen as
(faid hee) to weane an infant
the nurfes anointe the nipples
of their breaft wight Aloës,
Succotrina, or other bitter
druggs: euen fo that we may
forfake all delicacyes and fenfualities haue an auerfion frō
them, loofe and altogether
forget their taft, that whatfoeuer in them pleafe, it is ne-

C 2 ceffary

ceſſary that we impoſe a certaine amercement, a mulct, a
fine, on our vaine deſires, and
let vs change the hovvers of
our ſuch pleaſures into the
practice of rigour, and auſ-
terity, & at that time wherein
we vvere accuſtomed to vſe
a fond and diſordinate recre-
ation, vvee vvith all humility
to examine the ſharpenes of
thoſe torments vvhich our vicious, and deteſtable life de-
ſerueth. I knowe not by the
ſuch deliuery of this good
Father vvhether he did not
recotd the Cuſtome of the
Hebrewes, vvho inuited their
freinds yea made a ſolemne
                        feaſt

feaſt on the day of vveaning
their Infants, either to rejoyce
for that leauing a leſſe nouriſhment , they accommo-
dated, and applyed them-
ſelues to the vſe of ſolid
meates and full of juice, and
of ſtronger ſabſtance , or to
inuite thē to vnwóted meates,
according to the preſident .
For we vvell can vvery com-
modiouſly , & vvith ſingular
propriety transferre & adapt
this example to the inſtructió
of our ſpirits ; if ſo that vve
vvill weane our ſelues from
the milke of niceneſſe and
ſenſuality , and make an irre-
concileable diuorce from our

G 3   vices

vices, vve inuite our selues, &
are guests to such a like feast,
as vvas that of those Saincts,
and religious, of whom *Philo*
in his cotemplatiue speaketh.
They met at this banquet: the
first, principallest and most
delicate messe consisted of
beautifull and vvell sauoured
fruites of sapiéce, of wisdome,
vvhich vvas presented, and
set before them by an eloquét
expression, and Preaching of
Prophecyes, and commande-
ments of God as pure vessells
and vncontaminated, altogether vnspotted. Their recrea-
tion, and mirth, vvere consola-
lation; their pastimes, their
delights,

delights, vvere austerity; their
dainties, their jonkets, their
curious faire, their sensuali-
tyes, vvere abstinence. Their
spirits setled, and vvell tempered vvith such juice, vvith
such liquors vvere soe ordered
iu a sound and firme tranqui-
lity, to attend their more then
happy contemplations . To
speake in generall termes, this
exercise, this practise verily is
in effect very conuenient, &
agreable to our duety, but in
particular vvee haue yet neede
of another to accomplish the
cleansing and puryfying of
our soules, vvhich vve call
pennace: by meanes whereof

our foule returning it felfe
into it felfe vvill by diligent &
moft ferioufly attetiue, fearch,
finde the feuerall blurres and
fpotts that ftaine it and make
it deformed , yea, and vvill
expunge, & take them cleane
away . Now fince fo it is that
this pennance ought to be as
an entrance and preface of a
good , and perfect life , and
that by meanes thereof vve
may be purifyed, vve are with
greate folicitude, vvith fingu-
lar care frequently, yea, and
daily to put it in practife . For
fince that vve haue determi-
ned, and refolued to frame,
raife and refidence of the Diuinity,

uinity, it is neceſſary, and our
duty that vvee vvash it, yea
& againe vvash it throughly
vvith this water of Purifica-
tion, and let vs conceiue that
Ezechias addreſſed his vordes
to vs vvhen he ſpake to the
Leuites, ſaying : Encline your
eares vnto me with attention,
and ſanctify your ſelues, make
cleane the houſe of God, and
rid free his ſanctuary of al
vncleannes. We vvould that
our ſpirit be the Altar, our cogitations and mindes, his of-
ferings, our prayers, his pre-
ſents; and shall wee ofter it in
a place ſtained and contaminated ? Would not he forth
C 5 vvith

vvith pronoūce vnto vs what
he deliuered vnto the *Iewes*, by
the voice of *Malachie* ? I haue
not set my heart on yee, nor
vvill receiue sacrifices from
your handes : for you are replenished vvith filth, pollu-
tion and abomination. But
againe vvhich is the vvay vve
shall runne , how shall vve
begin this so good, so faire, &
so profitable practise? S. *Chry-
sostome* herein is our Leader,
our teacher, and our Maister,
and imparteth vnto vs a rare
instruction and a sound do-
cument. It is expedient, yea
necessary (saith hee) that vve
contemplate, and hence know
                                    our

our selues, and taking compassion, taking alas! pitty of
our misery that vve crush,
quash, quaile, and make out
heart droope : that vvee haue
our heart fully fraught vvith
expressed acknowledgments
c four sinnes, and the rest of
our actions all-rendred to a
true, sincere, and singular humility. The foule, filthy, and
brutish concupiscéces finding
our soules voide of the grace
of God, haue there taken their
place, and residence, and haue
puft it, and made it obdurate,
hardened it, in such manner
that nothing that good is can
(now as the case stands) haue
ingresse

ingreſſe, if ſo that firſt wee
should not by the hands of
a ſtinging contrition haue
ſquealed, and compelled it. In
ſomme had vve not aſſwaged,
abated the puffing vp of this
bladder all ſwolne with winde:
this ſpirituall liquour, this
holy oyle of conſolatió would
neuer finde acceptance, or admittance. Preſumption hath
been that firſt aſſoulted the
Angells, and hath after ſet on
the feete of man fetters alas!
ſnares, ginnes. Here lyeth the
buſines that we as with a
heauy waight are held continually affixed to the luſtfull
affections of the world which
                                ſeaſing

feafing on our defires in our felues, and making vs beleiue that vve liue for this vvorld onelie, hindereth yea ftayeth the flight of our foule which doth make directly to heaué. How shall we be able to acquit and free our felues? By cafting our eyes on our life, by reflecting thereó, weighing, vvell pondering our foulenes and deformity, and the innumerable afflictions, and miferies which daylie take vs at vnawares, vnprouided. If the Iuftice of God very indulgent in our behalfe should not afford vs fufficient enough to diflike our felues ; or becaufe

that

that we are very nighe to our
ill estate, in so much as vvee
cannot discerne it: let vs addresse our contemplations on
so many Millions of men,
which are in being, or haue
been: let vs well cosider what
a poore thing was their life,
and yet how this litle is enui-
ronned, is incompassed and
assiedged with paines, sadnes,
and anxiety, which are the
fruits of their sinne. The
common speech, the daylie
discourse of all liuing men, is
it not of their mishappes, is it
not a continually vttered có-
plaint of their misfortune &
misery. But is it not according
to

to reason that we should seeke
out of our selues (culpable,
vitious, and tranſgreſſors as
wee are) a ſubject to diſpleaſe
and contriſtate vs. Our con-
ſcrences: ordinarily ſpeaketh
to vs, & doth repreſent whether wee will or no, & againſt
our wills the regiſter of our
treſpaſſes: which is what *De-
mocritus* ſayed, that he had
heard the voice of malice ,
which of its owne accord accuſed it ſelfe : Furthermore
the diuine iuſtice or elſe the
fatherly ſolicitude , and care
of God continually sheweth
vnto vs ſcourges , ſometimes
he inflicteth on vs ſome
ſtripes

ſtripes to ſtirr vs vp, to awaké vs, to raiſe our ſelues vp out of this miſerable ſloath . If there be nothing els that may winne vs to hate our ſelues, & deteſt our ſinfull life: let vs caſt an eye, or let vs looke about vs, and ſeriouſly conſider this hideous, terrible and dreadfull image of death, which our ſinne hath contracted on vs . It followeth vs euery footſtep, cótinually, and euery vvhere, aſvvell by ſea, as land; it goeth a ſhipboard vvith vs, it rideth behinde vs, and no leſſe doth it leaue vs then doth our ſhadow. In all the courſe of our

life

life vve fly it, and it fo falleth
out, and in effect it is that
vvee goe daylie nigher and
yet nigher to it. It is it which
in a momēt cutteth in funder
the thred of our defires and
vnawares violently fnatcheth
away vvhat we haue amaffed,
gathered together vvith in-
duftrie, much care, & greate
toile; & at length it depriueth
vs of our felues, conueig-
heth and ftealeth vs avvay
to the vvorld. Let it be that
his image be fo depainted fo
gaftly, fo grim to be contem-
plated on, at each corner of
our life, the bridle of our vnjuft
vvills:

wills: let vs giue back and decline, beholding such a ☜ hirlepoole, such a swallowing gulph, such a bottomles pitt. Bee it that we be so farre engaged that we cannot looke back, that we are not able to make our returne; at least it will warne vs of the danger and to abandon and vtterlie forsake this base and heauy burthen, to suddainely and cheerfully rise with a liuely, & sprightlie leap out of this precipice, out of this desperate danger, and cast our selues and recommend our selues into the plaine, faire, & florid place which we discouer on

the

the other báncks , the other
fhore , which is the life of E-
ternity which attendeth to receiue vs . But if fo the reflec-
tion on this temporall and
corporall death fufficeth not
to make our thoughts encline
yea fall of : but when fo that
we fhall confider, and ponder
vvell that vvhich vvee are
threatned vvith in time to
come, vvhich is the fpirituall,
ghoftly , & euerlafting death,
vvho is hee among vs , vvho
is not taken vvith feare, and
horrour, vvho doth not mife-
rably tréble ? Horrible death,
fince that they whō it feazeth,
on vvhom it layeth his hands
dy

dy eternally, and yet they
dye, ~~but for~~ beatitude, to
ſepiternall happines of which
they are for euer and euer
depriued: they liue euerlaſ-
tingly, and yet ſoe liue they,
as that they liue to no other
end, but for anguish, greifes,
and torments, which they are
appointed to ſuffer, and for
euer to endure. Alas! cannot
vve figure it ſo ſo gaſtlie,
ghoſtly and horrible that the
beholding it's countenance
might not eſtrange vs, and
driue vs avvay farre from
it? In lievv of a dart that it
beareth in it's hand: let vs
vvith fire and flames, let vs

arme

arme it vvith tortures and
pinfers but contraryvvife vve
adorne it vvith all choice of
garments and the moft fe-
lected : for to vvinne its fauour. Wee trick it vp, vve
decke it , vve fet it forth to
make it to be more gracious
to vs , and it our freind : vve
erect'altars to it, and we make
no feaft, nor take vve any ioy
or comfort , but vvhem fo
that vve confecrate and giue
vp our fpirits . And when ?
whé we bath our felues in the
worldly delights , or rather
when we plunge our felues in
the infernall floods, depthes of
                              forget

forgetfulnes vvhich extinguish that of celeſt.all fire
vvhich is in vs and make vs
heauy, ſleepy, ſtupiſie vs, and
turne vs to a brutish nature.
And yet notwithſtanding we
ſay that vvee liue, and reckon
them not among the dayes
of our life but vvhat we paſſe
in ſports, merriments and
laughters, but further in vices
and wickednes. VV e are truely
like vnto Boat mé who turne
their backs to the shore where
they vvould arriue to. We
make reſemblance to recoile
and auoide death, and vve are
euen breathleſſe haſtning
thither according to the manner

ner of our life. Since such like
is this our state let vs fixe our
eyes directly, and steadily on
it, & on so many other rocks
as there are, vvhich vve must
crawle ouer in this voyage, in
this pilgrinage, to the end that
the feare, yea the terrour may
vvorke a good effect in vs, &
make vs discreet and vvise.
And let vs consider that vve
are now so hurt, and as it were
euen crushed and bruised, that
if vve be saued by an especiall
grace of Heauen, with greate
difficulty can vve oscape ship-
wracke. Looke on contrition
vvhich ought to make our
soules it's place of residence;
obserue

obferue bitter repentance
which should fend throbbs
frō the bottome of our heart.
It is that which should raife
in vs a hatred of our felues, to
reconcile our felues to God,
and to change our vicious and
vncleane life to that of purity,
and all whitenes. It is it which
calleth vs to iudgment in our
felues, for feare left vve be
cenfured by the iudgment of
aufteritie. For who is he whofoeuer he bee that can iuftify
himfelf? But indeed it fufficeth
not that we haue fully yeileed
our hearts to fuch compunc-
tion, and repentance, it is expedient, yea neceffarie that
vvee

wee manifeſt our ſinne and
the iuſtice of God , to the
end, that wee may receiue his
mercie and conſolution Wee
therefore are obliged, and ne-
ceſſarie it is that to make our
ſorrow acceptable , we make
him a right-vvorthy amends,
and that ingeniouſly we confeſſe our errour, our treſpaſſes.
For ſince that it vvas his vvill
and pleaſure that his bounty
which he might haue reſerued
to himſelfe ſhould be impar-
ted yea and liberally powred
forth to all his creatures ,
ſithéce that he hath created all
things to manifeſt his glorie,
and that the vſe of our life is

D   not

not beſtowed vpon vs but to
glorifie him, vvee cánot better
repaire our treſpaſſes againſt
him in corrupting the vſe of
our life, then in profeſſing and
manifeſting that he hath created vs to a good end , & that
vve our ſelues haue turned
our ſelues to euill It is expreſ-
ſly neceſſary, certainely it be-
hooueth that wee declare him
liberall, and vve vngratefull,
that vve publiſh his goodnes,
and that vve are bad , vnworthy and vvicked; that vve pro-
nounce his iuſtice , and our
ſinne , that vve ſignify and
proclaime our cóplaints our
moanes, and his pitty, his có-
                          miſe-

miseration; that vve make a
solemne protestation that all
the ill vvhich is in vs, cómeth
by our selues, and solety is
such through our ovvne
fault, and that the good vve
hope for proceedeth fró him,
For if vvce be silent after that
vve haue recognized, called
into our remembrance our
transgressions, and our greiuous delicts, this taciturnity,
this vsing no wordes draweth
vvith it beleife, & an assurance
that vve perseuer in the same
manner of life which we were
vvont, and it cannot but appeare, that vve approue by
such silence that vvhich vve
D 2   vvould

vvould confeſſe and freely
blame & condéne our ſelues.
In like ſort *Tertulian* exhorting vs to this acknowledgmét
ſayeth: That vvee doe not có-
feſſe our ſelues to God, as if ſo
that our tranſgreſſions vvere
hidden from him, and that of
them hee were altogether ignorant: but ſince that confeſſion is conſaile of ſatisfaction, vvhich diſpoſeth vs to
reconciliation, reconciliation
to mercy, and mercy to eternall and euerlaſting life. Be it
the ſatisfaction on vvhich wee
attend, & vvhich vve expect,
is deriued from his grace: by
meanes vvhereof onely, vve
ought

ought to be, and may be reſtored to immortality, nor is grace giuen to any but to him who acknovvledgeth his offences, nor is it beſtovved but by him who hath the foueraigne power. It is needfull thē that the vvord vvhich he beſtovved on vs to glorify him be employed to manifeſt our miſerie: ſince that the confeſſion of our ſinnes iuſtifieth the bountie and goodnes of God vvhich vve poſſetted, before that it vvas peruerted in vs. It is expedient yea neceſſary that vvee pray vnto him and beſeech him ſuppliantlie for his pardon, ſaying that

D 3 ₁vvee

vvee deserue ill, that in his
povver it is, and that he ought
to punish vs, in such deliu ry
of our selues vve giue testi-
monie of his power and his
iustice. To this scope did *Esay*
call on vs, vvhen he called out
with a loud voice, Goe yee on
the other part, and accompa-
nie the sanctified, and goe yee
I say along with them who
liue, offer vp to God your acknowledgments, your con-
fessions. Oh vvhat a comelie
and beautifull thing it is, vhé
that he who is found faultie,
deliuereth vp & manifesteth
his forrow, and true repentance! reallie it would be a
                                        glory

glory vnto vs, if so that vve
proueso couragious to aduow
publiquelie our transgressiõs,
and to shew that as vve vvere
first in falling, that we are the
first to repent vs. But their
taketh roote in vs, and sprin-
geth an ill bashfulnes vvhich
is imprinted in vs as a skarre
of sinne, which maketh vs
more slow, and dull to put
this in execution. Hence is it
that Iesvs-Christ by the
instruction he left vnto his
holy church applying himself
vnto this our infirmity, our
weakenes, and to the frailty
and imbecillity of those vvho
by the recitall of our enor-

mous

mous errors might be hurt,
and suffer, sometimes very
strange, is pleased to ordaine
that we do dispose, & discouer
the secrets of our soule in the
bosome of him to whom he
hath power to binde & vnbind
vs, to lose vs, and vnlose vs,
and to apply vnto vs the grace
by which we are freed and re-
deemed. From this Sacramét
we receiue a maruailous benefit, & singular fruite, when
so that it is worthily adminis-
tred, when so it is well applyed
and made good vse of. For he
to whom is committed the
dispense of this grace, made a
ghostly father ought to bring
comfort

comfort to the distresse which
he is made acquainted with
in the examinatiõ of our life,
the same reguard & affection
which a louing & charitable
Father doth in the behalfe of
his young and tender child
afflicted with sicknes , who
doth not onely bring him as-
sistance and remedy, but also
doth winne him to an hope of
his recouery , and therewith
doth dayly and hourely comfort him . It is his office and
duety in compassionating our
miserie , and taking on him
the fardle of our trespasses, to
releiue vs euen then vvhen we
vvere vveake alas ! feeble ;

and like to finck vnder the
heauy burthen at half wayes
iourney made. To him hath
God shevven the patterne, to
him hath he giuen the example: which as *Esaie* notheth he
in his ovvne perſo came forth
firſt and loaded his back with
all our infirmities, and hath
borne on his shoulders all
our maladies. After that hee
hath imported, and yeilded,
vnto vs this conſolation, he
ought to direct vs and chalke
out to vs the vvay of trueth,
and vvith the inſtrument of
the Word of God vvherein
he is verſed manure and im-
proue the faith vvhich he had
ſovved

sowed in vs ; vvhich through
the ill condition of the Land
vvhere it is, hath alvvayes need
of care and hand of the La-
bourer. For vvee are much
alike to a vvherry vvhich by
ftrégth of oares goeth againft
the ftreame , vvhich be it that
rovvers do neuer fo litle leaue
of their paines and repofe ,
they are farther caft backe in
one hovver , then they
promooued , then they gott
forvvard in one vvhole dayes
courfe. The end and confum-
mation of this holy Action is
that the holy Ghoft operating
in vs, grace is deliuered and
pronounced vnto vs , is ob-
taind,

taind, ingrafted, confirmed &
accomplished, by this Minif-
ter and inftrument of the
Church: which is vnto vs a
certaine pledge and teftimony
that as wee are loofed,forgiuē
and made pure in this world,
by him to whom the graces
of God are cōmitted:euen fo
shall we be found in the other
by him who gaue him this cō-
miffion, and authority.

Then after will there not
be remaning ought but to
humble our felues in the re-
cognizance & acknovvledg-
ment of the grace which vve
haue receiued; Thefe thinges
by our owne meanes are
                        hardly

hardly to be arriued to, vvith
great difficulty to be atchei-
ued by our felues, vvell may
we admire, and much, but we
shall be like the example of
our aūciēt fatheres, how they
carried themselues in this
practife of holy pennance.
Thou mighteft haue feen thē,
faith *Tertullian*, proftrate at
the feete of Altars couered
with fackcloth, foyled vvith
ashes, to weepe to bewaile, &
bitterlie to bemoane their
tranfgreffions and to exact,
and with great earneftnes euē
to extort & wreft, as it vvere,
forciblie G o d s mercy. But
thefe are meanes and reme-
dies

dies to which vvee haue no
recouise but with all our
might, for that the bridle of
this bashfullnes which vvee
conceiue of vvhat is good,
doth extenuate , nay dravv
backe, yea suffocate, stifle what
soeuer good in vs is awake-
ned, promooued & inforced.
And what worse is , a pittifull
and commiserable thinge this
is , that to what the voice of
the Holy Ghost, the coun-
saile of Prophets the example
of the holy Fathers cannot
draw vs vnto, the ire, the
wrath , and vengeance of
God doth traile vs and dray
vs . Wee couer our face vvith
a cloth,

a cloth, but it is when so vve
cannot do ought else; & ashes
on our heades, but it is to dif-
guise our selues before the
wrath of God who seeketh vs:
wee make our recourse to the
Altar, bnt our end is to hide
our selues frō his hand which
pursueth vs. Rebells, mali-
cious, and lewed seruants that
vvee are, we neuer giue our
due honor to onr Maister but
vvhen so his cudgell is ouer
vs, and threatneth vs: vvee
cry him no mercy, but euen
vvhen he is euē on the pointe
to cut our throats. It is therefore necessary that vve de-
meane, & conserue our selues
so

so humbly before him, and in his sight that we abandō not, & chase avvay through vaine and presumptuous phantasies that grace vvherewith he hath cleansed, and againe purified vs. Obserue vvell, after vvee shall haue so gathered as by hand the vices, vvhich are as it were the brambles, the briers of our soule, and that vve haue vvatred the feild of our consciences vvith our teares, and hence it became softned, moistned, and mollyfied by such like manadging thereof and that the clouds discussed, dissipated and cleared, the sunne of Gods grace vvill
beginne

beginne to appeare, yea cleare
shine aboue, and ſend forth
his gliſtring beames, & bring
comfort, and vvarmeth to it.
Thou muſt take good aduiſe
herein, that thou maiſt ſovv
there ſuch a ſeed vvhich happily and maturely may produce, may bring forth for its
fruite a diuine and immortall
life. This ſpoken of ſeed is our
ovvne proper vvill vvhich according as it happily or vn-
happily shooteth out his yoũg
branches, produceth, bringeth
forth good or euill fruites, as
euill actions, bad vvorkes.
Much to this purpoſe deliuered, *Theagas* the *Pythagorean:*
that

that this will vvas as it vvere
the hand of the foule whereby it mooued, and difpofed
all thinges either to good or
euill. Which felfe fame the
Scripture teacheth vs. That
God from the beginning formed man, and left him to his
owne counfaile, his owne will,
and to himfelfe: hee hath fet
before him fire and water, that
hee might choofe either, make
election of vvether. That
which can addrefle this vvill
to good is right reafon which
is the fquare, line, and rule
which conducteth all thinges
in the vvay, and to the end
vhich God created them.

That

That a man may with more
facilitie diftinguish and difcerne it, and that it may be
more eafy to him to doe vvell
then to faile and fall, and that
he should alwaies be anxious
and perplexed vvhat to determine, to refolue of: befides
the law of nature which he
hath giuē him and imprinted
in him , he hath furthermore
giuen him his law, by vvhich
hee may be conferued , if fo
that he vvill obferue it,and to
vs who liue in his beleife more
ouer and aboue by his law &
his precepts he hath further
benignelie enlarged,himfelfe,
for he hath beftowed on vs
his

his grace, vvhich foe long as we conferue it, operateth fo much in vs that wee will doe nothing but vvhat is conformable to his cōmandements, & by confequence anfvvereable to right reafon. Attend! this rule of well-doing doth not ought confift on acute propofitions all taken vp with fubtilities, and alike thofe of the Sophifters, to finde out which, and difcuffe them a whole entire age would be required. All this fcience, all this knowledge is comprifed in two words or fayings. *To lowe God with all his heart, and his neighbour as himfelfe.* And

not-

notvvithstanding to make
the vvay-more easy to vs ,
and to leade vs as it vvere
by the hand in all our workes,
in all that wee goe about, wee
haue certaine precepts to
examine, and to make euen
each of our Actions, and to
finde the manner, and meanes wherein is found the
conueniency and dependan-
ce of that which vvee vvould
put in execution and pra-
ctise. This conueniency, this
correspondency , or rather
disposition of our spirit to
conduct vs thither , vvee
call by the name of Vertue.

But.

But becaufe vertue changeth
and taketh on it a particular
dominatió, a particular name
according to each Actió wherein it appeareth : it feemeth
to mee much to the purpofe
& anfwereable to the fubiect
wee now treate of, to falute it
by the principall kinds which
for the moft part reprefeht
themfelues before our eyes.
The Philofophers began and
tooke vpon them to teach
vertue, in perfuading valour,
greatnes of courage and ani-
mofity but I defire to follow
their difciptine vvhofe liues I
willingly would make my
patterne, and imitate. *Philon*
                            the

the Iew ſpeaking of the Religious who vvere ſcattered
here and there in the deſarts
of Egipt, and with great perfection of ſtate of life attended contemplatiō, deliuered,
that as a principall thing on
their ſoules, temperance as a
good, ſolide, and certaine
foundation, on which they
vvere aftervvards enabled to
ſeate, place, and eſtabliſh all
ſorts of Verrues. It is expe-
di nt therefore, and concerneth vs hence to take our beginning For if *Plato* mooued
by ſome reaſons compareth
our ſoule to an horſe vvhich
is to be managed and ridden
by

by an expert Quiry, a skillfull horseman: it it necessary that before he spurre , that he be bitted, to the end that he may courb him , and hane him in command, and at his vvill, & pleasure, when the horse may take heed to leape out of the lifts & boudes, that hee may thereby be enabled to maister him , and turne him att command vvithout hazard of beating himselfe , vexing himselfe, dauncing, leaping, and running his chaunce and danger. Wee call this temperance the authority , and povver that reason ought to be endowed vvith on the vnbridled

bridled defire and violent affections that our will beareth
towards vaine delights, and
fenfualities. It vvill be then
as it vvere the courb of our
foule, or rather it vvill ferue
vs in liew of an inftrument fit
to take of the skimmings
which raife themfelues vp in
our foule through the heate
of our blood, to retaine and
conferue it alwayes vnited
and conformable to reafon,to
vhich it ought to proportio-
nate it felfe , and not to accommodate it felfe to fenfible obiects, vvhich are fett
before it, prefented vnto it;
giuing no vvay to them, but

E contra.

côtrariwife the bufines should
be fo managed , as that they
should altogether ferue them
conforming themfelues to it
and reafon, vvhereof it ought
to be entirely compafed. And
as for paffions on vvhich
ought temperáce to take care
of, to keepe in compaffe of
reafon, the most ordinary is
a foule concupifcence, which
poffeffeth vs, and as it vvere
bevvitcheth vs vvith carnall
loue , and maketh vs feeke in
the conjunction ordained by
God not the benediction of a
long and happy pofterity to
fubrogate and appoint in
our places feruants of our
Creator.

Creator. But a brutish pleasure, & infamous senfuality, vvhich blinds our foule and drunckenly befotteth our fpirits. God hauing endovved, enriched, and heaped on man so many other perfections, he vvould yet further to accomplish him: adde that vvhich in all his Diuinity is more admirable, making him in a manner Creatour of himselfe. For euen as hee created the world to contemplate and difplay his vertue, his goodnes his infinite vvifedome in his ovvne workes, fo was it his pleafure that mā should beget his like, that he likewife might

E 2 be

be feene in his workes, and
that he loue and cherish that
which hath had his beeing
from him; to this end hath he
giuen vnto him a woman for
his affociate and companion
to this worke. Hee hath done
more, for it hath pleafed him
that man heretofore bond-
flaue, and in the povver of
death should looke for a
time, for a day when as a
brách, an offpring of his pofterity should be brought
forth, who was to bee the
Sauiour and Redeemer of
the world, as hereby inuiting
vs to vfe religioufly a fainct-
ly vnion, vvhich vvas to
apply

apply it felfe to the minif-
tery , to the feruice of his
redemption Since that now
in thefe times the vfe , and
practice of this conjunction
is not expresfly neceffarie
for our fafety; vvhich is entirely acquired ; and that it
is left vnto vs as a lavvfull
intemperance, if fo that vvee
cannot decline it : let vs make
vfe thereof as of a remedie
of infirmitie vnder the authority of diuine Law, to affwage,
abate , yea and extinguish
the côcupifcences, & burning
flames which shoote forth in
our bodies . And fince the de-
E 3   fire

sire vvhich casteth vs out of
our selues, cannot induce and
vrge vs on, enforce vs to the
loue of God, as vvell ought
it to doe : let it at the least cõ-
taine it selfe in the chast bosome of her, whome God hath
destined, appointed for companion. Let vs consider well,
let vs be solicitous and vigilant that vvee make not our
selues vessells of vncleannes;
let vs be tenderly carefull not
to soyle, pollute, defile the
temple of God (since that hee
deigneth, he voutchsafeth to
bee in vs, & to allodge in vs)
vvith the impure commerce
of those impudent, who a-
busing

busing their bodyes, doe likewise infringe, misuse, yea
corrupt all sortes of Lavves.
For they trāsgresse the Lawes
of God vvhich commandeth
chastity; the law of Nature
vvhich prohibiteth to make
that common, vvhich is destined to one, vvhich is appointed for one solely; the
lawes of Natiōs vvhich haue
recommended and brought
in marriages; and the right of
familyes, transporting and
vnjustly transferring the labour and paines of any one
to a strang heire, to such an
one vvho is nothing to them.
Without all doubt from this

E 4　　vncleane

vncleane and vnbridled concupifcence iffueth forth, and
is deriued as from a liuelie
and plentifull fpring as it were
all mifchiefes, as vvell publique as alfo particular . For
when fo that this foolish loue
is figured , and formed in our
foule vvhich cherished and
nourished vvith exceffe, with
fuperfluitie & idlenes maketh
his increafe ; and euen as a
thinne, fprightly, and fubtile
poifon difperfed all through
our veines hath befotted ,
and as it were brought our
fenfes to a Lethargy , & hath
ftupified, benummed our lim-
bes : it chafeth away reafon &
aban-

abandoneth it farre from vs, and impoſing on vs a furious rule , yea a meere tyranny, tranſporteth vs to foolish and outragious deſignes , & courſes . Doe vve not ſee it ſupplant the greateſt Kingdomes , and Empires to fail to ruine? See vvee not that it deuoureth in one day the riches and conqueſts of many ages? That it maketh vvay to all ſorte of vnjuſtice ? doth it not procure jealouſies among brothers , quarrells betweene Fathers and ſonnes ? but the vvorſt of it's effect is an vncertainty vvhich it bringeth in parents and deſcendants.

E 5 For

For polluting the nuptiall bed
it robbeth from the children
the loue and charitie of their
Father; which cannot be con-
serued othervvise then in the
opinion vvhich the husband
ought to haue of his vvife her
chast life: & it likewise taketh
avvay the piety of children
tovvards their Fathers, which
depends on the same consideration. Now the bonds of affection, good vvill and charity being lost in humā kinde,
vvhat remayneth to containe
them in amitie and ciuill society? vvhat is left them to
conserue them vnited in the
seruice of God, & obedience
of

of his Commandemēts? This
sinne is, as sayed one of the
Auncients, the Deuill's gate;
vvhich stealing os vs his vo-
luptuousnes euermore cat-
cheth hold of vs vvith nevv
heates, vvhich enflame, and
set on fire all our soule, and
soyleth it vvith smoke, bere-
auing it both of sight and
iudgment to guide it selfe to
any good vvorke. Let vs part
from this foolish loue as farre
as vvee can, vvee ought to
chase it, and detest it as the
true and reall poison of our
spirits. But contrary-wise we
lowdly call vnto it how farre
so euer it be from vs: vvee
                    inuite

inuite it to take it's recom-
pence : the prizes of honour
are not but for his instru-
ments : all the beautifulleſt
& rareſt witts are not hindred
ought , that they may not
peint, and deſcribe, and ſet
in order each feather of it's
wings, to the end it may fly
more ſwiftly , and more to
pleaſe throughout the Pal-
laces of Princes. A Chriſtian,
I meane him who vvould arriue and ſoare to this happy
contemplation , to vvhich
vvee prepare him : vvill lay
aſide, and deſpoile himſelfe
of all his deſires and vvills
and practiſing à continuall
con-

continence vvill endeauour,
if poffibly it may bee, to
conferue this treafure of Virginity, wherein is found a
great purity of fpirit, and
perfection of intelligence and
knovvledg: for the fpirit of
God is principally commu-
nicated to them vvho con-
ferue it. Which miniftred occafion to *S. Ierome* to fay after
Varro that the price & value of
Virginity was Diuinatió, fince
that Diuinatió is no other thé
the knowledge of the future
trueth, vvhich wee acquire
by cómunicating with God:
that which wee cannot obtaine, if we cotaine not ourfelues
free

free and pure from all terrestriall and brutish affections. But if as aboue hath been sayed our infirmity our frailty surmount our reason: Let vs so carry our intemperance that vvee make it lawfull and excusable, in the right vse of that remedy, vvhich God hath prescribed to our infirmity: and be it so vvith vs that vvee resemble those of the Primatiue Church, of vvhom *Tertullian* reporteth that there vvere noe males but for their females With reuerence, with due respect to this conjugall society, and let it a conjunction of spirit and vvill, a com-

munion

munion of faith, and of Religion: vvherein there is nothing of propery or particularity, no not their most secret thoughts. It is vnion (as sayeth *Themistius* the *Platonick*) which ought to be altogether, and in all respects one & the same; as vvine and vvater vvhich once mingled cannot for euer be seperated.

Behold vvherein vvill be discouered the principall effect of this temperance : to practise humane kind, in sobriety, and to detest an infamous gurmandizing, and vile and filthy sensuality, and ouernice daintinesse . Vertue

there

there is not retarded nor hindred but by seruants and gal-
ley-slaues : such cupidityes ,
such euill - seasoned desires
seldomely fall out ~~but~~ in in
genuous spirits . But bee it
that within the memory of
time there haue been such
monstrous *Sardanapalians* who
make a God of their belly, the
euen common voice and out-
cry of the people doe detest
and abhorre them; and so insuf-
ficiently are they scorned and
reprooued by the vulgar, that
it is not necessary the Philosopher should employ his
time in further reprehensiōs
of thē, or to take any paines
                          therein

therein at all. It is moſt certaine that ſuch ſpirits ſuffoca-
ted, ſtifled amõg their curious
and dainty dishes cannot
breath out any thing which
may ſauour of generoſity ,
or ought celeſtiall, which may
render them capable of the
contemplation, to which wee
inuite them, & call them. Euẽ
ſo vvhen *Philon* deſcribeth the
life of thoſe ſingularly good
Religious of Egypt, he there
vvell obſerueth ſuch a nota-
ble ſobriety : that it vvas not
poſſible that the body ſo nourished could bring any incõ-
uenience, or impedimẽt to the
ſoules braue & glorious actiõs.

Wee

Wee vvill vſe therefore food,
& other temporall, caduque,
and feeble goodes, to ſuſtaine
and repaire the infirmity of
the body ; as a neceſſary inſtrument of the ſpirit . Nor
vvill vvee doe ſo vvith it as
Princes vſe their garments
of great ſolemnity, and pub-
likly ſhewing themſelues ,
which for that they are ſo
heightned , & emboſſed with
Goleſmith's woike and skill,
and ſo charged and embro-
dered vvith iewells; that vvith
difficulty are they able to
mooue themſelues, ſo great is
their burthen; wee vvill make
an euery-day-ſuite, a vvork-
day ſuite,

day-ſuite, vvhich vvill yeild,
bee plyant, and as eaſy as wee
would deſire it to bee.

There is another ſubject
through vvhich the ſoule is
no leſſe hindred, it it vvas by
theſe it's other paſſions. It is
Choler, vvhich to ſpeake
truely of, is no other, then fiñe
and curious flower of folly,
and madnes. This is the paſſion which dazeleth, yea blin-
deth vs in an inſtant vvhen-
ſoeuer therewith vvee are ſur-
priſed, & it maketh all things
to appeare vnto vs as inuiro-
ned and all compaſſed about
yvithin a Cloud, farre otherwiſe, and farre different from
what

from what really they are: &
which is the more dangerous
guesse by howmuch the more
they who ècertaine it are great
persons, are fully franght with
puissance, povver, and authority. For the choler of Princes, which is assisted, backed,
and seconded by force and
might passeth and maketh
it's vvay like a thunder-bolt,
vvhich vvracketh, worketh
runce, and splitteth asunder
before it hathshewé his flash
of lightning, or hath been
heard. And euen as the thun-
detbolt breaketh the svvord
without hurt to the scabberd:
euen so it punisheth without
entring

entring into consideration,
and knowledge. In so much
as their actions for the most
part are attended vvith an
vnquiet, vnsetled and vnpro-
fitable repentance; not being
of power to doe more, then
to wish that which is ill done,
had neuer been donne. For as
Pindarus sayeth God himselfe
hath no other povver of what
is passed, but to forget it : &
euen so they are often con-
strained to repent themselues
at leasure, of that which they
did very speedily & hastily.
But to represse this impetuous & vehement rage : it is
necessary

necessary vvee forme, and
make vnto vs a moderation
of spirit, vvhich vvee enstyle
by the name of Clemency;
through vvhich our vvills in-
considerately mooued and
put on, to vvill ill & mischeife
to others, and to desire reuenge; may be retained and
repressed. When so that it
shall be once ingrafted in vs,
and that therewith vvee be
vvell seasoned through an exquisite obseruation of our
manners: it vvill temper vs
sweetly, and graciously, that
by it our reason vvill be defended & strengthned against
the assaults of so vnquiet most

vn-

vnpleaſing, offenſiue, and
ſtrong impreſſion, vvhich is
choler. It will giue time, and
leiſure to judge of things maturely and by weight & meaſure: to take counſaile of our
freinds; and it vvill diſwade
vs, dehort vs from giuing cre-
dence & beleife to our ſelues.
To this purpoſe, and end it
vvill infinitely ſtand vs in
ſtead to perſwade our ſelues,
that wee cannot be hurt but
by our ſelues, and that of the
injuryes done by others, there
is not ought extant, or in
being in vs : but vvhat wee
vvillingly retaine. For if our
demeanour, and actions be
                           harme-

harmelesse, and pure & intire:
our life sainctly & innocent,
can the venimous & enuious
tõgue of our neighbour chãge
it, can it hurt it? but if so that
at any time vve determine &
propose to our selues to liue
ansvverably & conformably
to the opinion of others, whé
vvill it bee that vvee shall
haue foũd the meanes to giue
satisfaction and content to
all the world, and to each one,
and to please the good and
bad at once? let our iustifica-
tion be presented before God,
and our selues and our conscience being cleane and vncontaminated, vnspotted, vn-
pollued;

polluted; there is not ought
which can,offend vs,or doe vs
mifcheife. Thou wouldst
wrong mee in mine honour;
& thinkest to bring false tes-
timonie to robbe mee of my
life,and greiueously to misuse
mee,and to iniure mee:I haue
God,men,and my conscience
witnesses against thee, vvho
yeild vnto mee fecurity, and
iustifie mee. Likely it is that
thou maist earnestly entend
and vvill mee a mifcheife, but
I am not sensible thereof if I
will not.Thou carryest away,
and by force takest away my
goods, all this doth not shake
mee:Either such was my state

F   that

that I vvas not true owner of
them, or I poſſeſſor of them
ſo youg that I knew not what
belonged vnto them ; and in
concluſion if ſo that you had
let me alone to poſſeſie them,
yet could not I carry them
avvay vvhen I depart from
this my life. It cannot be o-
therwiſe but that I leaue thé,
or they mee : why should I
conceiue more greiſe, & take
more to heart the one or the
other? Thou hurteſt my perſõ,
thou beateſt me & vvoundeſt
mee ; and behold a ſouldier
who returneth all-cheereſull,
all-ioyfull from the combate,
bearing his arme in a ſcharfe:
he

he holdeth his wound more
deare then his life; if thence
he haue a flash ouer the face
vvhen he beholdeth it, hee
is vvell pleafed therevvith, if
fo that his arme be maimed,
hee goeth not a fteppe but
with joy that he is fo glori-
oufly marked. They are not
then the vvounds which are
foe troublefome, irkfome,
and fmarting, but the occafions by vvhich vvee receiue
them; it is the honour or dif-
honour which from them we
deriue, vvhich thy bring vs;
and nothing is efteemed for
it felfe, but for the end for
vvhich vvee doe it. Let vs

F 2   en-

endure all for the honour of
God , and for the safety that
may hence redound, and that
vve may acquire through our
patience : and that vvhich is
called ill, vvill turne to good;
that vvhich sometimes seemeth bitter , vvee shall proue
svveete. The patience vvhich
this moderatió of spirit shall
bring to vs , and endovv vs
vvith vvill render vnto vs a
secret testimony , a vvitnes :
that wee are faithfull seruants
of our Maister : that vvee decline not or duety, that vvee
spare not our selues a jott to
obey him : that vvee fly not,
auoide not ought labours or
                              what-

whatſoeuer paines to execute
& fulfill his cõmandements.
There is not any thinge truely
vvhich beareth vvith it more
honnour in this vvorld, euen
according to the opinion of
Pagans: as is that it to know
to pardon. The lawes permitt
to each one to purſue by Iuſtice reuenge of iniuries re-
ceiued:to giue grace,remiſſió,
and pardon it appartaineth
onely to a Soueraigne Prince.
If ſo that then thou vvilt be
King and Soueraigne of
thy ſelfe: pardon freely. For
the glory of a Chriſtian conſiſteth principally on this charity: by vvhich it obligeth his
F 3 neigh-

neighbour to loue him, and to
vnpester and free himselfe
from this corosiue & bitinge
desire of reuenge, vvhich doth
not onely gnaw like a worne
the hearts of them vvho are
infected but doth ofté mooue
them by day, and keepeth
them watchfull in the night.

Then shall our spirit com-
pose it selfe to this equality:
not to let it selfe to be tranfported by an hatred, grudg
and rancour, and ill vvill. And
from hence vvill cófequently
follow an other right vvorthy
difpofitió of the foule. which
is a modesty & moderation;
which bringeth vvith it a certaine

taine feemliues , a certaine
comelines to all the actions,
and carriages of the body,
wherevvith it rendreth testimony of sincerity, and good
vvill. Vertue which is of more
power then are all others, to
make vs sociable, and to con-
ciliate, to comme, to gaine
the freindshippe of them, to
whom either our disposition,
and nature, or our fortune, or
our election doth combine
vs, conjoine vs . This gentile
and vvell-becomming fashiõ
is so agreable and pleasing to
men, as nothinge more; and
doth euen vvrest from them
that vvhich force cãnot com-

    F 4   maund,

maund, cannot the maister
of, cannot acquire. For it re-
quireth nor exacteth any su-
periority ouer others: but by
reason; vvhich is a certaine
kinde of weapó more sharpe,
and more cutting then is that
of iron, or steele it selfe. But
these proude, surly & disdeig-
nefull vvho crossly looke on
the vvorld, vvho are pusfed
vp to their very skinne, and
admire their traine as doe the
Peacocks: doe vvrong euen
so to reason it selfe vvhé they
make vse thereof; in such
manner cloathing it, that
they dispoile it of its grace,
and render it odious. And belieue

leiue that it is very difficult
that they approach nigh this
faintly Philosophy, vvhich
resideth amidst the graces,
vvhich vvaite on it, and en-
uiron it on each side. *Tertul-*
lian desiring to informe and
teach vs how much meeke
sweetnes, and simplicity con-
ferreth to vs to dispose vs to
the receiuing and admittance
of guifts, and perfections of
the Holy-ghost, sayth: that ex-
pressely hee appeareth vnder
the figure, & forme of a doue,
toshevv vnto vs that he in-
habiteth not but in thé, who
are vvithout gall, as the doue,
and are replenished vvith

F 5   grace

grace and meekenes. But for
that ofte it happeneth through
our infirmity, that thinking
to fly one vice, vvee fall into
another: vvee ought to beleiue
that since that vvee are not
well confirmed & established
in vertue, imagining to containe our selues in humility,
that vvee fall not in a remis-
senes of courage vvhere vve
ought to breech it out, & bed
it. It vvill not then ought be
impertinent, or out of our de-
signe, and purpose to adde to
vvhat vve haue deliuered of
temperance and mansuetude,
meekenes, certaine consider-
rations vvhich may raise vs
to.

to a kinde of ſtrength and
ſtoutnes of courage, when ſo
that vvee ſhall haue neede
thereof, that which principally will ſtand vs in ſtead, &
ſerue vs to hold vs vpright and
ſtanſt againſt all vvhich pre-
ſenteth it ſelfe to daunt vs &
diuert vs to the obeyings of
God's commandeméts. Wee
ſhall haue on one part a teme-
rarious and raſh preſumption
vvhich vvill further vs to deſire more thé God hath called
vs vnto: vve vvill generouſly
ſet againſt it this conſträcie &
ſtability. Happy ſucceſſe and
good fottunes mooue vs to
ſingular pleaſure, euen to pro-

fuſe

fuse laughter: our chaunce will
promise vnto vs greatnes, and
magnificence: wee vvill not
for all this chaunge our visage
and countenance. Wee vvill
disdaignefully looke, & ouer
the shoulder scornefully, on
the presents of fortune; like
vnto apples whichgrowe nigh
the Lake of Gomorrhe, which
are beautifull, and florid in
their colour, but let them be
touched neuer so carefully,
and tenderly, they all fall to
ashes. If not vvithstanding
reason doth dictate vnto vs,
that vve ought to accept of
them, wee vvill vse them with
great equality and euen téper

of

of ipirit, and happines and fa-
cility of cuſtome and demeanour, not valeiwing our ſelues
at any higher rate vvhatſoe-
uer. Wee ſhall be beſett, and
on the other part haue afflictions, dangers, enuyes, and
pouerty; vvhich according
to the vulgar eſteeme & iudgment doe envvrappe, côtaine,
and imply all ſort of euill, &
all kinde of miſery. Principally againſt theſe ſuch like
enimyes, this vertue muſt re-
inforce, and giue vigour to his
arme: it is againſt thê that he
make good his paſſage, if ſo
that he will winne the goale,
　　　　　　　　if he

if he vvill arriue to the marke
vvhich is propoſed. But if wee
apprehend not a feare and
are not poſſeſſed therevvith,
and that vvee ly not before
vvee ſee the face of our enimyes vvhat hurt can fall on
vs, what miſchiefe can they
doe vs ? They will deſpoile
vs of our goodes; wee ſhall
goe the lighter, & leſſe clogd:
for the price, the game, the
reward belongeth to him who
firſt arriueth to the goale, and
it is he who ſhall enjoy a loger
ſpace and time of immortall
and euerlſting good, whoſo
ſhall firſt come thither. Shall
wee be afraide to looſe or
                    baggage

baggage & luggage, to gaine
such a victory ? Behold the
breach made, the passage opé,
our Captaine is there within,
who calleth on vs : and doe
vvee amuse; study, and attend
earnestly to shoote against
him who taketh vs by the
cloke, and wee put our selues
to hazard of being made prisoners in the hands of our eni-
mies , who will compell vs
both to loose our cloke , as
also our honour , & the fruite
of all our paines , all our labours. One threatneth vs with
death, and what is that which
wee preferre before it ? Wee
haue cloathed this fraile,
weake,

weake, and mortall life, but
to pay tribute & to difcharge
the through-toll at the gate
of immortall life .   They
are good tydings , good
newes to heare one fay, Pay, it
feemeth vvee are at shore. But
vvhat is death , vvherevvith
the vvorld doth fo much af-
fright vs? vvhat hath it of fo
terrible a condition , that it's
prefence occafioneth vs to
turne our face & contenance,
& forfake the field of vertue,
to make hait avvay and hide
our felues vvithin the tren-
ches , or in the berryes and
holes of vnmalynes, vnvvor-
thynes, bafenes, and cowar-
diſe?

dife? If wee esteeme it ill and mischieuous, it is such to vs because vvee apprehend such like, or for that others accout it at such a valiew. Haue vve euer heard vvhat vvere the complaints of them who couragiously layed downe their liues, either for the honour of God, or for the seruice of their soueraigne, their King, or for the defence of their Coutrey? Hath there been in any age a Natio so barbarous, soe meanely endowed with humanity, & as one may say, so farre from the Sunne & his irradiatios, his bright beames, whoe

doth

doth not recommend, ard
highly extoll with glory and
renowne the valour of them
who haue sacrificed then liues
for the publique? Hath not
the memory of their posterity
taken them oue of their robes
to make them reuiue and liue
in the remembrance of men?
And when we come to reckō
the partes of the life of man,
account wee the time which
they haue employed in their
repaſt, their eating & drinc-
king aud sleeping? & if so that
we make mention of them,
and ſett thé downe in writing,
one accounteth principally
the dayes, in which with great
animoſity,

animosity, and singular courage they haue fought for vertue: It is then but through error and deprau̅tió of iudgment, that you giue the denomination and name of life, which is no other then death since that it perisheth vvith leauing records, and memory of it selfe: that which you enstyle death, and call it vnder such name, is true life, for that it is vvhich giueth vnto vs to bee, and remaine eternally, to laft for euer and euer. Wee must not once reflect on how longe we liue, but how vvell wee liue. Death neuer commeth too soone, if so it be ac-

com-

companyed vvith honour.
Yet notvvithstanding death
is not to be lesiened, nor des-
pised for the sole and onelie
opinion of others, and for
the honour vve acquire in our
vvell dying: it is for the loue
of that other life, to vvhich
vvee come vnto all-happy.
The *Druides* presented somewhat of the immortality of
our soules; this made them
more generous and famous
then vvere all the Nations,
and people of the Vniuerse,
of the vvhole vvorld. The des-
pisedeuen to laughter and all-
scorne to be sparing of their
liues vvhich they valievved

no

no more then the vvagging
of a ftraw, or the toppe leaues of a vvillovv tree, or the
leaues of a birch tree, vvhich
are carryed and returned like
Apfen leaues, euery vvay. The
Philofophers though they
flighted them, and mocked
them, yet deliuered, that they
vvere happy in their errour.
But vve fay that they vvere
fortunate in their vviledome,
to haue had a taft of this o-
pinion : to haue founde by
chance, in darkenes the place and meanes of vvorldly
felicitie : to haue founde
the counter-poifon the Anti-
dote

dore which chaseth away and
dissipateth feare, and dread,
true venome of our soules;
which maketh our courages
arid, dry, withered & decayed,
and languide . But we now
further instructed in a better
schoole then vvere they, wee
doe not onely know, but wee
stedfastly beleiue; and we doe
not onely beleiue, but wee as
it vvere enjoy this second im-
mortail life. Wee haue a spirit
which is seated in the midst of
our soule , which deliuereth
vnto vs, & dayly resoundeth
nothing els in our eares (if so
that we will giue our attentió
to it) but the notes & melody

of

of this life to come. It is this
voice that so many Millions
of Christians, haue followed
against all afflictions & whatsoeuer torméts, the Enseigne,
their captaines displayed cou-
lours, vnuanquished, powring
forth their blood with all rea-
dynes and vvillingnes, in all
the parts of the vvorld, as the
true & pure seed of faith. It is
the trúpett which hath moo-
ned thé forcibly to this cóba-
te, from vvhence they returned all bloody, but yet victo-
rious, triumphát, & crowned.
If an ambitious honour doth
cast on the strangest and des-
peratest perills of vvarre; if
this

this our passion, and affection
to be esteemed, valiewed, and
honoured by them in vvhose
sight vvee are, doth spurre vs
on, and giueth viuacity, life,
and spirit to the race & course
of our actions: vvhat much
more may vve hope of that
vvhich they haue acquired?
They haue not beé onely honoured in the time of their
liuelyhood, but vve euen reuerence their ashes after their
death, their very bones are
holy, and sacred, the memory
of their life is yerely renewed
by deuout commemorations,
and prayers, vve render them
honour in our thoughts, vvee

humble

humble our cogitations before them, they being placed
in a great degree of honour in
the Church of God, as those
who haue found grace in the
sight of our Soueraigne Lord.
Wee therefore ought not to
want courage to effectuate &
bring to passe those things
vvhich are good and saintly,
since that the very wicked are
for the most part so valourous
and hardy to put wretched
practizes, yea such as are most
detestable in execution. For
it is in this patience, & in this
is this force of courage, in this
fortitude that vve enter as mé
in triúph into the kingdome

G   of

of Glory . It hauing been deliuered vnto vs by *Tobias* that
excellent and faintly Oracle
that he , Lord, who ferueth
thee vvith all his heart, if his
life come to the proofe and
tryall , shall vndoubtedly be
crowned . Hence is it that the
Scripture fayeth , that this
good Father being in a miferable captiuity forfooke not
this notwithftanding, the way
of trueth. And to fpeake vprightly vve cannot iuftly af-
cribe vnro our felues the names of Chriftians : if vvee caft
of , and abandon the Croffe;
which is bequeathed vnto vs
in lieu of all manner of vvea-
pons,

pons, vvhich is the token, and
marke, which IESVS-CHRIST
hath beſtowed on vs, to diſtinguiſh vs when wee ſhall arriue
to him, which is the watch-
voord which giueth warrant,
and teſtimony that vvee are
his owne. Wee haue no other
meanes to make known that
vvee are inſtructed in his diſ-
cipline, but by this Patience
true mother of all other vertues. Euen ſo ſayed *Theodoret*
that the Martyrs made all haſt
to tormēts, as to the ſchoole,
exerciſe, and practice of vertue.

  It ſucceedeth in order, and
proper place that vvee vvell
          G 2   obſerue

obferue, and take care, hovv
vve ought to behaue, and gouerne our felues, in the vfe &
difpéfatió of the goods which
God hath pleafed to conferre
on vs. The rule which is pro-
pofed vnto vs, and the difpofition, habitude, and cuftome
which wee admitt to make
good vfe thereof, is called Liberality. Well novv, the firft
precept vvhich vve ought to
learne : is to acknowledg,
that all the goods vve haue,
we hold them fró the bounty,
and grace of God, vvhofe ordinary practice is to doe good
to all the world, and to povvre
forth on vs his blcffings, although in no fort we doe de-

ſerue them. That which he ſo
prodigally doth diſtribute &
diſpenſe, is not to the end vve
ſhould keepe it locked vp, or
that wee ſhould let gold or
ſiluer become muſty, vvhich
haue no vtility, no cõmodity,
or profit in them, but in their
vſe: but to the end that as he
hath created vs according to
his ſimilitude, wee might imitate him in doeing good to
our neighbour, to the vtter-
moſt of our power. And really
vve haue much more reaſon
then hath hee: for vvhat he
beſtoweth, he giueth of his
proper, & to thẽ who haue no
meanes of retribution, nor
to cõferte ought to his good.

But vvee manage the purse of
another: we diſpéſe the goods
of our God, vve beſtow them
on perſons who cannot onely
repay vs , but lend vs as much
in our exigence, and neceſſity.
And vvhē ſo that they should
proue inſoluāt & not paying:
God by vvhoſe commande-
ment vvee giue it, doth anſwere vs by them, maketh it
his owne debt , he chargeth
himſelfe not onelie to returne
vnto vs the principall, but the
vſe, the double, the threefold,
the hundreth-fold. Further
wee ought to conſider that all
theſe ſpoken of goods should
beare a proportion to our
                              wants,

wants, our neceſſityes: and
that by the right and law of
nature , they appertaine not
vnto v s,they are not our owne
in proper, but vvhat vve haue
neede of for entertainement
& ſuſtaining our liuely-hood.
The meaſure of our good is
heate, cold, thiſt, hunger. Yf
the cuſtome of the Countrey
where we liue,and the faſhion
and manners of our fellovv-
Citizens & neighbours inuite
vs to ſome particulat thinge,
ſome property, and delicacy:
we muſt not too auſterely , to
ſeueiely, reiect, and refuſe, nor
too nicely, & vvith too much
curioſity affect them. Rather

wee should obserue well, and
take sufficient notice in what
degree of honour God hath
estated vs among men, which
is suteable to the rake in which
we are borne, or called vnto; to
the end that wee may accom-
date goods to vs , not our
selues to goods. Whē we shall
haue attēded seriously on the
discouery of vvhat we whant:
wee must let the rest passe and
bee layed aside, & be attētiue
and vigilant to dispose it will.
And that vvhich may ad-
dresse vs thither, is to examine and finde out the desert,
and need of them to vvhome
wee will dispente it: For proportion

portion and fymmetry is that
principally, which redreth, &
maketh the worke holy acceptable, and gratefull to God:
who hath difpofed all thinges
by meafure, and hath giuen vs
reafon, & difcourfe for bouds,
as a paire of Compaffes to
mach fitly and to difpofe or-
detly our actiós, to the likenes
of his . If fo that I giue my
goods to one who hath of thé
no want, and that one who is
really poore dye at my feete,
this liberality to the rich, is im-
prudence, is want of difcretió,
and foe farre as concerneth
the poore vvretch, is homi-
cide. If I leane my Father, &

G 5   mother

another in want , to help a
ftranger : the order of true &
naturall affectiõ is peruerted,
and my deed and what I haue
donne loofeth its grace , and
lufter. It is neceffary likewife
that you obferue to vvhom
vve vvould thefe our good
workes be applyed: fome vrge
vs more then others : to thefe
we may doubt whether vvee
may giue : thofe others doe
fnatch violenty from vs our
good vvorke. But vve ought
to haue principall regard, to
giue nothinge that belongeth
to another. For they who take
away forcibly frõ one to giue
another : are abho.ninable in
                                       the

the sight of God : their almes,
and offrings haue ill sauour
before his presence:he turneth
his eyes from them . Hence is
it that the Wiseman sayth:the
offring of him who presenteth
to God his iniquity , is full of
filth & nastynesse, wee ought
to make great accounte of
this vertue, and forme it , and
fully imprint it in our minds,
our spirits , as being replenished vvith a spirituall grace;
which may conferre much in
leading vs the right and ready
vvay to our safety , since that
it can accustome vs freely &
liberally to distribute our
goods to them vvho stand in
need,

need, and to giue almes in the
name of him vvho hath bes-
tovved them on vs: *S·Augustine*
hath no feare to say, that Almes deedes is a second Baptisme: For that euen as vvater
extinguisheth fire, almes-
deeds doth redeeme & quéch
sinne. It is faith *Saint Chryso-
stome*, the freind of God, which
obtaineth of him all vvhat
it desireth: it enlargeth and
freeth prisoners: it calleth
back the banished: and it im-
petrateth, obtaineth by suyre
and prayer grace for the condemned. The hand of the
Poore is the purse of God. Is
there any thing vvhich vvee
vvould

vvould of him ? Let vs lay
downe our money. We cãnot
fo vvell employ our money,
and to fo good vfe, as to put
it into the banck of God. Hee
vvill affure vs them not onely
on earth, and ouer all its con-
tinent, vvhich is all his owne:
But aboue in the heauens,
and eternall beatitude wherevvith he vvill configne and
inueft vs . Then vvhat is the
caufe vvhy vve become of fo
fmall iudgment, and bee fo ill
aduifed to let ruft, as will gold,
as alfo filuer in our coffers,
and to haue a minde alvvayes
bét to heape money on money
in meane vvhile let the time
of

of our cōmerce and traffique
to glide and paſſe by, and
that all this which vve heape
vp, is it other then care vpon
care? Vndoubtedly all theſe
riches which are waited vpon
vvith toile, and paine through
their greatnes, which cannot
be further meaſured: or other
then a Cage of gold, & priſon
of ſiluer to their Maiſters &
poſſeſſors to hold them faſt
tyed and chained to the earth,
and to bereaue them of the liberty to aſpire to heauen It is
water caſt on on Eagles wings
to the entent ſhee ſhould not
fly towards the Sunne. In ſuch
like manner they who vvill
                                    caſt

taſt the fruite of contemplation,& ſoare and penetrate to
that *Soueraigne* good where
the race of the ſoule is to make
his goale, and reſt : Let them
not be encombred be entangled the leaſt that may be ,
vvith the filthy mudde of riches;vvhich are of naught els
but earth, hovv great eſteeme
ſoeuer vvee make of thé. And
yet not with ſtanding for this
duſt vvee kill one another : it
is it vvhich ſtirreth & maketh
contentions of our bodyes &
minds . For this haue Citties
bandied one againſt another;
armyes prepared and encountred : it is the plague of ciuill
ſocie-

society.: it is a strong vvater which disuniteth bretheren, behold further, seperateth the father from the childré. There it is very necessary, yet further more to plant in the affectiós of men a fourth & last barre, to retaine and hinder vs, that wee desire not that vvhatsoeuer appertaineth to another; & teacheth to giue vnto each one what belógeth vnto him.

This vertue wee enstyle Iustice: which cósidered at large, & somevvhat more generally cótaineth in it all other kindes of vertues. And it's office as *Lactantius* teacheth, is to vnite men vvith God: Secondly to

make

make one man accord vvith another in amity &freindship; vvhich are two things much a-like in proportion. For if it cōtaines in the office to which God created vs , vvhich is to feare him, to loue him , and ferue him, and to be good to our neighbours: vvee cannot but bee in the good grace af-vvell of God,as of men. Now to weigh and deliuer this ver-tue more particularly , and in that vvherein it difpofeth vs to liue iuftly and lavvfully a-mong men , it may be de-uided very commodioufly & aptly into Three parts .

The

The One , to liue honeftly
vvithout breach of the Lawes
of God, & the Countrey. The
other, to doe noe injury or offence to anv body in deed, or
word . The Third, to giue to
each one vvhat appertaineth
to him. That which might be
deliuered on this fubject ,
would exceede the boundes,
& limitts which we haue pre-
fcribed to this fmall treatife.
It shall fuffice vs to fay that
the principall thinge which is
recommended vhto vs by Iuftice: is to keepe our faith in
all our affaires; not to confpire
or practice by deceipt, and
craft, ought; but to goe on purely,

rely, candidely, and openly in
busines. For besides that faith
is the knott, and cómon band
of amity , and society of men:
it is moreouer a pledg that
God hath giue vs, in communicating himselfe to vs: where-
fore we may imagine , that
vvho soe abuseth this pledg
among men , vvill easily a-
buse this pledg which God
hath giuen him. And really
hee that shall sett before his
eyes, the Law which is giuen
vs by God : the iudgment
vvhich he hath denounced ,
and proclaimed to vs : the
paines and inflictions vvhich
are

are prepared for the wicked:
vvill hee be so foole hardy
at all to deceiue him, whom
the Lavv commandeth that
he loue as himselfe ? vvould
he in deceiuingh his neighbour defraude and beguile his
soule of eternall beatitude, e-
uerlasting blessednes, vvhich
they cannot be partakers of
vvho communicate, and con-
uerse with the Father of Lyes?
Trueth , verity commeth
from heauen , and deceite
is the daughter of darkenes:
all paintings, all disguising,
and counterfeitings , all lyes
are the subtile guiles of the
Deuill:

the Deuill: and he vvho fo en-
tertaineth them, and maketh
vfe of them contracteth and
bargaineth with the maligne
fpirits, & is made bond-mã to
finne. It is therefore requifite
that all our actions be reple-
nifhed with fincerity, and loy-
alty and truftines; but principally it concerneth them who
are called to the gouerment
of people, and vvho are guar-
dians or Feoffees vpon truft
in the vvay of iuftice, to apply
it to particular perfons. It is
not fit that they should car-
rie, as the Iudges of the
Egiptians trueth hung about
their neckes; it is neceffary
that it

that it be imprinted , yea engrauen in the center of their hearts , and in the middest of their lipps: and that neither loue nor hatred make the balãce vvhich they hold in their hands shake, or mooue at all; but that right reason onely make iustice beare downe by weight against iniquity, that iustice preuaile , against impiety. Vndoubtedly mã could not haue made in his conscience a more sure vvitnes of his approbation, then that he pleaseth himselfe and taketh comfort to be iust & vpright. For he vvho loueth iustice is according to Gods heart , is a

man

mã of God. The light sendeth
forth it's beames, and maketh
all clearenes to a iuſt man, &
to a man of vpright heart. The
part of a iuſt man is alike to
the firſt riſing of the Sunne:
whoſe light by degrees encrea-
ſeth, and becommeth alike
to the ſplendour and clearnes
of noone day. The Wiſemã
could not cõpare iuſtice more
aptly, and more properly thẽ
to the light. For euen as the
light ſhineth not, irradiateth
not for its ſelfe, but to giue
meanes of ſight to others:
euen ſo this vertue forſaketh
it ſelfe entirely: hath no regard, nor intereſt but the good
                             and

& benefit of another ; hauing
no other aime and fcope but
to counite and entertaine our
felues mutually , one vvith a-
nother by meanes of good
vvill, and fincere and vpright
affection.

When this vertue is arriued
to its perfection, it maketh an
eafi paffe to charity, and iuftly
may it vfurpe the name. For
it hauing vnited & conjoined
vs together it teacheth vs to
efteeme the flesh of one and
other , as being members of
one body, or as compofing
the body of one felfe fame
head; and it leaueth vnto vs a
charitable affection, vvhich is
                          the

the very fouldering and faft
tying of our foules. For euen
as we fee in the conftitution of
our perfon, our parts cópofed
in fuch manner, that the re-
moteft part mooueth it felfe
in an inftant according to the
difpofition, & affection of the
other : and if the foote fuffer
hurt, and endure paine, vve
looke downevvard, & imme-
diatly put our hand to it, and
fet our vvhole body to affift
it,and releiue it. Euen fo in the
conjunction of the myfticall
body, and in the faintly Congregation of the faithfull of
vvhich vve are all members,
the fpirit ofGod which ruleth,
H and

and gouerneth vs; inftructeth
vs, that for our conferuation,
we ought to cherish one another, and that vvee efteeme
our croffes,and our good for-
tunes common to vs all, to
cótribute one to another. For
our Chriftian iuftice deth not
onely binde vs to the acquit-
ting vs of our ciuill and poli-
tique duties which may occurre amongft vs;but likewife
this naturall obligatió which
tyeth man to man with good
vvill and mutuall charity.

Now it remaineth that this
iuftice doe conjoyne vs to
God, & that it produce more
excellent effects, vvhich hold
our

our foules vpright, peaceable
and capable of Diuine vvill,&
as vnited to the loue of euerlafting beatitude . Which
thinge it doth by the guifts of
Faith,and Hope.For after that
vve are cleanfed of peruerfe &
foule paffions, the vvhich our
foule had receiued by the vniõ
thereof vvith the body ; and
that vve haue in fuch manner
limitted our vvills on euery
fide that it cãnot turne it felfe
to ill:yet oughtwe to aduance
it and further it to its goale,
shew it the way of its iourney,
and conduct it to the place of
it's repofe . Now as vve are
plunged in the darkenes, in

the deferts of finne, & botto-
meles depthes of perdition:we
cánot fee our marke without
light,nor finde our way without guide,nor hold,and lift vp
our felues without a ftaffe or
croutch. Our light,our guide,
our croutch is the reuelation
vvhich hee hath giuen vs of
his grãce: it is the fpirit by
which hee doth communicate
it vnto vs, & he himfelfe doth
vifite vs; for that vve are fo
weake,and feeble, that we cánot goe to him.

Wee call faith : the right &
found affection from vvhich
vve receiue that vvhich he deliuereth, and vve beleeue it
firmely,

firmely, and through vvhich
vve iudg of him in goodnes,
and fimplicity of heart, and
wee digreffe from our felues.
Herewith we hūble our fefes,
and we digreffe frō our felues,
to giue credit and faith to
his trueth: let vs acknowledg
our infirmity : let vs aduow &
confeffe his puiffance, & Omnipotency : let vs adore and
admire his effects his vvorkes
foe often reiterated, fo often
repeated, to regaine our fafety,
and to deliuer vs from euerlafting death . When once
our foule hath giuen it felfe
ouer to be rectified, and difpofed by this beleife, & hath

H 3   receiued

receiued this faintly impreſſion, and feale of the vvord of
our God : then doth it perſpi-
cuouſly and moſt cleerely ſee
it's mark and bonds; and then
vvell deſcerning good vvhich
is propoſed to it, vvhich is ſet
before it , it is touched vvith
a certaine ſenſible apprehēſiō
of pleaſure , which mooueth
it forward earneſtly, aud continually to wish for the good
which is prepared for it, and to
waite on it . It is this hope by
meanes of which it foreſeeth
the hower of it's happines: by
which it is entertained in ex-
pectation of it's beatitude, its
bleſſing, and ſuſtained, and re-
in-

inforced, and made very powerfull & mighty against the
annoyes, & disquites and mi-
seryes which oppose & ouer-
thwart its way. Marke well the
how we ought to prepare our
soule, to render it capable of
it's felicity, it is necessary that
we behold it in its operations,
and that we contemplate it in
it's action, meane vvhile en-
joying this Soueraigne pleasure and content.

Wee must consider it tvvo
vvayes. One vvhen inuolued,
& inclosed within the body,
and detained in this inferiour
world: it notwithstanding is
ioyned and vnited with its

H 4   God

God its Creatour, through a
pure and faintly difpofitiõ, &
its good & charitable worke.
The other vvhen as freed, deliuered, & difarrayed, and dif-
poiled of the earth , and the
vvorld: it rejoineth it felfe entirely to its originall, & fountaine. In this firft eftate, and
being vve shall finde it to enjoy fortune, pleafure, and contentment: vvhich doth infinitely furpaffe all others vvhat-
foeuer they be, vvhich we can
defire in this vvorld: and yet
neuertheles is a thinge of nothing, in comparifon of that
vvhich vve vnderftand to be
prepared for vs in the other
                              life,

life , and vvhich our thoughts
cannot arriue to . For indeed,
as *Esdras* deliuereth , a man in
this life, in this vvorld cannot
comprehend but terreſtriall
things. It is not fitting, nay you
ought not, this ſayeth *Eccleſia-
ſtes,*ſearch curiouſly that which
is aboue vs: but thinke of that
vvhich God hath giuen vs in
command; for it is not neceſſary for vs to ſee that which
God hath concealed from our
eyes. Now the happines and
Soueraigne pleaſure of our
ſoule in this life: conſiſteth in
it's conforming & addreſſing
it ſelfe to that end , for vvhich
it vvas created: which it accó-

H 5 pliſheth

plisheth by deed , prayer, and
meditation . For God hauing
made vs Lords and Maisters
of this lovver vvorld , all the
parts vvhereof obseruing the
office,and motiõ that he hath
giuen vnto them , serue his
glory, & render testimony of
his puissance , of his greate
povver:it is necessary so long
as wee are there , wee beare
our part;and that for so much
as concerneth vs,and our particular wee discord not, vvee
spoile not,and peruert not the
accords, and compleate and
generall harmony , through
which the beauty of theworke
subsisteth . Hee calleth each
one

one to a particular office and
ſtate of being, and vocation:
he conſtituteth ſome Kings,
other Princes, other Magiſ-
trates, other priuate perſons:
where to ſpeake vvith the A-
poſtle , he hath conſtituted
ſome Prophets, other Euan-
geliſts, other Preachers, other
Doctors. Let vs looke to it,
and bee very ſolicitous to ac-
compliſh the vocation , and
charge vvhich is giuen vs. For
in being vvãting to diſcharge
vvhat vve haue receiued , vve
doe not faile onely in our
ſelues , but alſo vvee bring a
confuſion to the generallity,
& wee render our ſelues culpable

pable euen of the trespasses of
others . Whereas contrary-
vvise vvhen wee performe our
part iuftly : vve are like vnto
Muſitians vvhich beſides the
pleaſure of vvell and ſvveetly
tuning their voices , they are
taken vp vvith an incredible
ioy and delight at the agree-
ment, and encounter of the
voices of their fellowes, which
fall vvith their owne, vvith
accord , and cadence full of
ſweetnes, and o f melody. It
is truely a ſingular content to
doe vvell: there is novvorldly
delight like vnto it , nor ſo
great as the ſatisfaction and
hearts-ioy vve receiue in our

con-

confciéce for a good & praife-
vvorthy action, deed . Nothing mooueth the fpirit fo
farre forth vvith pleafure:then
the glory which is prefented,
and promifed to him, vvho
cóporteth himfelfevertuoufly
in his life.Not a glory vvhich
is fed vvith winde,and fmoke
vvhich folely affecteth the o-
pinion of men : but a glory
which makethvs sharpe fight-
ed , and to fee a farre of, the
croune which is prepared for
vs. Wee muft not no more
then may the champion, and
chalenger at wreftling ftay at
the shouts, & applaufes of the
people vvhich are on our fide,
and

& fauour our vvay, & courfe:
but rather they muft haften vs
to run more fwiftly towards
the garland of reward, vvhich
attendeth on our defert, and
victory. Let our foules be entertained, aduanced, and lifted
by fuch cogitations,   fuch
thoughts, and euen fo that all
our actions making their recourfe, and beeing directed to
this end may be replenished
with hearts comfort, and with
that contentment, wherein
confifteth our beatitude. Wee
cannot nor ought wee at all
times be bent, and employed
in the affaires of the vvorld:
After labour fucceedeth repofe,

pofe, which is notwithftāding
the true operatiō of the foule:
that is meditation. Happy are
they whofe calling is fartheft
of from the cares, and folicitude of affaires: and vvhom
God hath drawne from the
tempefts, and ftormes of the
vvorld, & hath brought them
as it vvere within a calme
hauen and quiet, to contemplate, & behold a farre of the
shippwracks of others. This
meditation confifteth not but
in the knowledg of the trueth,
and glory of God: which wee
ought to feeke after afvvell
to the contéplation, and exact
confideration of his vvorkes,
wherein

vvherein shine on all parts his
puiſſance and incomparable
goodnes, that by the ordinary
reading his vvord, by vvhich
hee layeth open the threaſure
of his wiſedome, and draweth
the curtaines of the heauens;
that he may ſoe as much as
our infirmity our vveakenes
can comport vvith, his diuine
and incomprehenſible Ma-
jeſty, face to face. As for the
workes of God they are truely
ladders which he hath erected
aud ſet vp euery vvhere to
mount vp euen vnto him.
For vvhich vvay ſoeuer vvee
conuert and turne our ſelues,
vve finde ſubiect to admire in
                        this

this vvorld . If vve caſt our
eyes downeward to the center
of the earth ; there diſcouer
vve ſo many veines of gold
and ſiluer, ſo many precious
Mineralls, ſo many fountai-
nes and ſprings of vvaters ,
that it moueth maruaile . If
vve behold the ſuperficies &
outward face thereof : we find
ſuch variety of herbs, of flow-
ers], of fruits , of liuing creatures, ſo many vertues, and
ſecret,&hiddē properties,that
are knovvne noe other then
to become hence aſtoniſhed,
amazed . But are not the Seas
leſſe to be vvondred at, regard had to their ebbe & flow,
the

the quantity of their fish re-
flected on, the diuersity, and
variety of their mosters which
they nourish thought on? The
aire fraught vvith Birds vvith
storme - threatning clouds,
raines, snowes, hailes, light-
nings and thunders, doe not
they suddenly take hold of vs
and extremely mooue vs to
astonishmét, or at least to ad-
miration? And when vvee lift
vp our eyes higher, and that
vve come to the discouery, &
perceiue the curtaines or pa-
uiglions of heauen extended
&displayed on the face of the
earth, and behold the splendour of the Sunne and the
                                    bright-

brightnes of the Moone, and
their coarſe ſo gouerned; that
vve obſerue the beautifull diſ-
poſitiõofſo manyſtarres, their
courſe, their effects and their
influences: doe not vve wõder
at them, are we not out of our
ſelues? And yet notvvithſtan-
ding all this conſidered in generall, &in groſſe it is nothing
compared to that vvhich vve
finde vvhē vve examine them
ſeuerally, in particular, and by
peece-meale. For then vve ſee
that the leaſt things of the
vvorld haue in their conſtitu-
tion, ſtate, & being a certaine
ſo maruailous prudence, and
wiſedome; that it is neceſſary,
                                    and

and that we are conftrained
to haue recourfe to heaué to
fearch out the Author, and
the Creatour. Let man be at
a ftand a vvhile, and that he
looke vvithin himfelfe : that
he onely enquire of his owne
ftate, and being, and vvhat he
is : hovv a litle humour doth
encreafe, and augment it felfe,
in fuch a manner that it for-
meth a body compofed of foe
many and, fo diuerfe parts ,
vvith fuch a proportion . But
let him not be fatysfied to fee
himfelle vpright on his feete,
yea euen vvith his face eleuated, and looking vp on high,
his eyes open, and moouing
                                    all

all his parts, all his limbs. Let
him but obſerue diligently &
diſcouer but his skinne a litle:
and let him but gueſſe hovv
his bones and his fleſh are ſo
vvell met, and agree ſo vvell
together, and ſo artificially.
Let him vvell obſerue how ſo
many Nerues and Muſcles
are deriued from the braine,
to the fartheſt and vtmoſt
bounds of the body, to binde,
looſe, & remooue all the parts,
to all ſorts of nations: let him
looke how ſo many veines are
diſperſed throughout the
whole body, to carry blood &
nouriſhment to each part : let
him

him contéplate hovvſo many
arteryes are conducted from
the heart, and are ſeuered to
accompany all the nerues, &
the veines; to bring into each
part the ſpirits as meſſengers
of it's vvill to the end to impoſe command to the nerues
to mooue, or reſt . But if he
come to diſcouer his ſtomack,
& hovv his life is entertained,
hovv the food vvhich thither
commeth is transformed by a
ſecret and incomprehenſible
vertue;hovv elaborated in the
ſtomak, it is ſeperated in the
gutts; hovv that vvhich good
is ſtealeth & ſlideth along by
the veines aſſiſtants to the
liuer,

liuer, vvhich is the shoppe of blood ; as the liuer doth discharge it's superfluityes to the gall,to the spleene, to the kidneys as it distributeth the blood vvithin the veines, as it sendeth to the heart to be attenuated and subtilized euen to the confectió, and making of spirits. If he see the motion, and respiration of the lungs vvhich refresheth,and tempereth the heate of the heart, if he see the ingenuous turnings and vvindings of the gutts : doth not he thinke that he is come from the clouds: and to see as vvell euery thing as those vvithout? But vvhen he

pon-

pódereth on the head , vvhich
is the treafure of the fenfes, &
the feate of reafon, let him cõ-
template as on other thinges,
what is that principall worke,
the eye , of vvhat excellency
it is , vvith how many filmes,
and membranes this fpirit of
light is garnished, & fupplyed
vvith, and defended, vvhich to
fpeake vprightly , is euen all
the pleafure of our life: he remaineth as it were aftonished,
amazed, and as it were out of
himfelfe , and yet not fo farre
tranfported, as vvhen he con-
fidereth the braine, and pene-
trateth it, where he perceiueth
and difcouereth the manner,
                              how

how the formes & images of
thinges are carryed by the
senses, as faithfull Messengers,
and interpretors, there to be
receiued and examined by the
common senses, & then there
to be disposed of, and to be
transferred to safe keeping in
the litle cabines or celles of
the memory. But that vvhich
doth mooue vs to admire
much more is vvhé we would
informe our selues vvhat is
this our soule vvhich mana-
geth and gouerneth all this
vvorke: vvhat we may deliuer
of this puissace, of this power,
vvhich hath such motions, &
strang actiós: vvhich vvaketh

I   vvhen

when wee sleepe, with such ease cōprehendeth al thinges, and findeth by discoarse the cause and reason of more secrets, & hidden thinges. Wee see it's effects, wee are sensible of it in our selues:but we haue not power to behold it, nor conceiue it. As sure as can bee in the contemplation of such things, be it that wee are raised and held vp by Faith:we finde that immediately we are conducted to be authour of such workes. And to speake sincerely so many maruailes dispersed through all parts of the vvorld: vvhat is it other then a booke opened, therein

to

to reade the greatnes ; and omnipotency of God, which therein is fo richly imprinted ? The euen fole and onely contemplation vvhereof might arreſt , and ſtay our ſenſes and ſpirits , and furnish them with plenty and ſufficiēcy of that contentmēt, vvhereon dependeth our felicity, our happines . It is thereon vve muſt ſtudy day , and night, and not to be cōtented to ſee the couer of the booke, but diligently the ſyllables, & leaſt points vvhich containe beautifull and holy ſecrets. In my iudgment it vvas a braue anſvvere vvhich *Socrates* maketh

keth métió to haue beé spoké
by S. *Anthony* the Heremite,
to a Philosopher, vvho demá-
ded of him how hee could
passe his dayes in solitarynes
vvithout bookes : who sayed
that he had no wát of bookes:
my booke is the vvorld : my
study is the contemplation of
nature; I reade day and night
the glory of my God, but I
cannot finde the end and vt-
most part. O happy life which
exempted from sharpe and
stinging annoyes which doe
weare and cósume our yeares
enjoyest this repose , and dis-
closings , and reuelations in
freedome, within the treasure
of Diuinity : which filleth the

desire of thy soule, of the knowledge of immortality: in so much as thou art trased, in an extasy, and euen giuest vp the ghost within the armes, and embracements of the e-ternall sapience, the euerlasting wisedome! These are the delights, the baites and alluremets which haue for threescore entire yeares retained *Acepsenes* amidst the desarts inclosed in a litle Cell. These haue been the baites and enticements which entertained *Simeon* all his life time vpon a colūne, vpon a pillar. In your iudgment vvhat vvere the wishes of such like people;

I 3　　who

who eleuated aboue the earth,
fwamme within the heauens,
communicating with the Angells;and beatifyed, and made
théfelues bleffed before their
death? vve vndoubtedly haue
the bloud about our heart
congealed,we are very fenfe-
les, or benummed , become
blockish, if we admire not
their happineffe,and take not
pitty of our mifery. Our fpirits
are much mortified,if wee có-
prehend not in this life,in that
contemplation , and in the
knowledge of this eternall
trueth: doth all our confola-
tion feate & ftate it felfe, doth
confift all our contentment,
                            and

and all our felicity & repose.

Now God vvho loueth vs as
his Children would not abā-
don vs to the darkenes of this
world;to leaue vs as blindfol-
ded to finde out a way, and
amidst his workes this his
owne trueth . But leauing his
spirit among vs, he hath deliuered vnto vs his v vord as interpreter of his will : wherein
we finde sure and faithfull ad-
dresses , to conduct vs to this
verity,this trueth,and to faci-
litate,and make our way easie
to the knowledg of it's his
maruaills.It is this voice which
is sayed to be embraced and
enkindled . This is the Word

which is termed light: which
Eusebius professeth to be alike
to fire. For that it doth not
onely heate, but it doth cleare,
and purify, it mooueth: but it
likewise melteth, it softneth, it
hardneth. Wee ought therefore imitate those good *Egyp-
tian* Fathers, whose liues *Philō*
describeth, who respiting their
eyes from the exteriour parts
of the workes of God, immediately did cast them on the
reading of Prophets, and holy
bookes, as on the commenta-
ries and interpreter of their
meditatiōs. For they are they
who haue far ther penetrated
this diuine wisedome; & hēce
are

are called by holy Scripture,
The Difcouerers, The Seers,
The Perceiuers. They haue re-
ueiled vnto vs the myfteryes
of Eternity; and not by humã
induftry, but by infpiration of
the Spirit of God : they haue
communicated vnto vs the
miracles of the heauens, and
laid open the way to wife-
dome. Towhich whé once our
foule is vnited, & hath réceiued
its forme and perfection : it
remayneth that it bring forth
its fruite, according to the in-
ftruction of the felfefame *Philõ*,
which is the property of each
perfect thinge.

The fruite of a foule medi-

tating;

tating; but rather it's child if wee will speake according to *Eusebius*, is Prayer: which doth conceiue in the inmost part of our thoughts, is brought forth out of our lipps in the same manner as a child conceiued in his mothers vvóbe: For the knowledg of God, & the sensible apprehension of his bounty which is imprinted in vs by vvay of a Saintly meditation doth promooue in vs this animosity, this courage vvhich *Mercurius Tresmegistus* doth call an invvard vvord: vvhich inly being well formed and assisted by the spirit, and body : forceth it selfe out-
vvard,

vvard, and aduanceth this exteriour vvord, vvhich vve call Prayer. Wee take not this prayer in the sense of customary prayers, vvhich proceed from our vveakenes, our infirmity, and ought to bee the beginning of all our vvorkes, & which vve vvould not haue kept as accounting it to be the last action of the soule: but for that by which vve expresse our passion, our affection bred in vs by our perceiuing, and knowing the goodnes and bounty of God: which after wee haue prepared our rogue by saintly thoughts

to

to him: it ruleth & gouerneth
&becómeth an inftrument of
his glory. Wherein wee finde,
if vve be therein faintly con-
uerfant, fo greate cótent. that
in our fpirit there is no place,
to receiue any other cogitatió,
any other thought. For be it
that we proftrate our felues
before him to implore his grace
or to requeft of him his benefits;or to render him thákes
for the dayly helps, and fauours, which continually hee
enlargeth vs with · our fpirit,
our foule is as it vvere out of it
felfe, and in an extafie, and we
perceiue his hande euen then
more prompt, more ready to
　　　　　　　　come

come to our affistance, then
are wee to call for it ; hee hath
long since giuen vnto vs this
assurance, that all vvhatsoeuer
vvee shall demaund of him in
a firme faith, hee vvill grāt vs.
let it be so that all howers, &
times, vvee, as our duty bin-
deth vs send forth our voice to
resound his laudes, his praises;
preaching and declaring his
meruailes , his vvounders ,
as vve are cōmanded, singing
the songes of his glory ; vvee
interchāgably answering one
another by Hymmes, and spirituall Canticles : our heart
leapeth in vs, & our spirit, our
soule doth lift it selfe vp to
heauen,

heauen, and vvith its contemplation, and thought vniteth
it selfe to its Creatour. When,
vvhat hovver, rather I may
say at vvhat moment may we
ceafe to turne the eyes of our
soule tovvards him , vvho
hath alvvayes his armes displayed, to receiue vs, his eare
ready , fauorable and indulgent to our prayers , vvho
beholdeth our vovves , and
benignely vnderstandeth thẽ,
and is not suspitious, mistrust-
full , but of the laudes and
praises vvee sing vnto him?
Are there affaires , or sleepe
vvhich may bereaue vs of
this pleasure, of this delight?

or

or rather may flily lurch , fecretly with drane our felues vvithdravv our felues from our felues , and make vs flug-gish, and dravvfy then, vvhen the fvveetnes of our fong, the feruency of our prayers doe collect our fpirits, and affem-ble them , to comfort and agree vvith the grace of the fpirit of God vvhich worketh in vs? Ought vvee to be deafe when fo that he toucheth the inftrument of our foule to accord it to the tone of his vvill and to fatisfie and fill vs vvith the melodie of this fvveete and perfect har-mony vvhich refoundeth,

from

frō the vniting our intellect,
our vnderstanding to his diuinity? O delights, ō immortall pleasure! vvho shall dif-
joine, vvho shall seperate
my soule from thee? vvho
shall violently snatch mee frō
thine armes, to carry mee away
from heauen to earth, from
splendour and brightnes, to
obscurity and darkenes: and
to seduce & peruert my senses
from purity, to impurity, and
mire, and filth? Liue then, my
deare soule, liue, and establish
thy selfe, & yet againe lay thy
foundation in the midst of
those diuine pleatures; vvhich
as pearles and diamonds are
　　　　　　　　　aban-

abandoned, and left to the vt-
termoſt parts of the earth, &
are at an eaſy rate, as cheape as
can be imagined, to thē vvho
haue the ſpirit, & courage to
goe thither to finde hem. Let
happines attēd this way, which
path to immortality, vvhich
ſvveetly leadeth vs, and vvith
pleaſure euen to the gates of
heauen; our God follovving
vs foote by foote, and holding
vs as it were by the ſleeue. To
vvhich place vvhen ſoe we are
arriued, vvee haue not ought
elſe to doe, but to caſt of this
garment which ſo much doth
hinder vs & ſuddainly to caſt
our ſelues in the midſt of the
abyſſes,

abysses , the vnmeasurable
depths of his glory . Where
filled not vvith pleasure , not
vvith ease, not with mirth, not
vvith delights not vvith vo-
luptuousnes, sensuality; but
vvith an vnspeakeable & incredible contentment, vvhich
surpasseth all that vvee are
able to say, yea euen to thinke
or imagine : vvee shall then
begin the race of this immortall life vvhich neuer hath to
haue an end : vvee shall enter
into this euerlasting beatitude, eternall blessing, from
which wee shall neuer depart:
we shalbe illuminated vvith
this glory more the celestiall,
　　　　　　　　　　which

which will neuer be darke or obscure.

But since thy last and most perfect felicity consisteth in the regarding of the face of the Father of light, vvherein wee shall see the spring & soūtaine of all goodnes, &beauty: and that hee vvill not that so longe as vve are entangled & enuironed by the darkenes of the world, that wee should see him face to face, but his back, and as it vvere passing onely. Wee will hold our peaces and admire in silēce thatwhichwee know to bee, but wee know not how: that whereof vvee cānot speake, but accusing our

igno-

ignorance: in so much as vvee
cã say, that it is nothing which
we know by sense, but a thing
which surpasseth beyód measure all perfection. Our senses
cannot pierce so farre, and our
spirit is so much more blúted,
and dully recoileth by hovv
much more it enforceth it selfe
and striueth to penetrate and
arriue to the extent thereof.
What remaines then for vs?
A most certaine hope that if
vvee conserue our selues pure
and cleane in this vvorld, and
make our selues vvorthy of
that grace & loue vvhich our
heauély Father offer's vs, per-
uerting not our affectiós & that
ho-

honour vvhich vve ovve him
to to earthly & vvorldly matters;vve shall one day enter as
children & heires of his glory
into the treasury of his hea-
uenly riches,and shall receiue
the fruite and ioy according
to his promises and of the
splendor and brightnes of his
blessed Eternity.

Laus Deo Trino - vni.